I NEVER HEARD
MY DAD SAY

A Journey of Identity and Wholeness

I NEVER
HEARD
MY DAD
SAY

A Journey of Identity and Wholeness

Cpt. John M. Arroyo, Jr., USA Ret.
and
Peggy Corvin, MPT

Praise for

I Never Heard My Dad Say

"Amazingly Transparent - Painfully Honest - Captain John Arroyo and Peggy Corvin team up to deliver "a one-two punch" for Jesus in the pages of this book.

As a fatherless boy who grew up to become a fatherless man, I could relate to every word that John shared from his heart as well as the wounding that he opened himself up about. The testimonies he shares, combined with the healing truths of the words of sacred Scripture, are a powerful tapestry of healing, hope, and transformation. "The Breaker Anointing" is truly upon and flowing through this broken man's life and ministry. I highly recommend this for any man or woman who suffered the pain of fatherlessness and needing the love and healing of our Heavenly Father.

This is a must-read to pass on to all hurting soldiers and veterans.

Well Done; You've Been Faithful, and I'm Proud of You My Son!"

Rick Menard- Ranger Ministries
Vice President- Maranatha Ministerial Fellowship
Author of *As a Son With His Father; Laying a Foundation for Spiritual Sons.*

"Through the pages of this book, I found myself drawn into a world where vulnerability is a strength and self-discovery a triumph. I Never Heard My Dad Say isn't just a book; it's a guide for those ready to embrace the truth of their own hearts and step boldly into a new chapter of life. John Arroyo has crafted a powerful book that will undoubtedly resonate with anyone seeking deeper meaning and personal liberation."

Danny W. Davis, Ed.D.
Founder at Equipped Servant
www.equippedservant.com

"John has had an incredible life that portrays God's power to save, redeem, empower, and deliver. His words are not filled with theoretical "fluff" and Christian jargon, but his heart is on display with all of his contagious passion for Jesus and His Kingdom of Freedom. This is worth the time to read, study, and put into motion.

Don't let, as John puts it, the "Weapons of Mass Distractions" keep you from experiencing true freedom. Thank you, John and Angel, for allowing me to be a small part of your story. Thank you for using what God has given you for His glory."

Pastor Dan Stanley, PhD
Riverside Assembly

"I Never Heard My Dad Say" is for everyone.

This book goes far beyond addressing the challenges experienced by those who have absent fathers. As one reads this, they find so much truth - the truth that sets one free and that freedom makes the way for genuine wholeness if applied. By the time one finishes this book, they'll discover that there's something else they've gained - a better understanding of and a deeper relationship with our Heavenly Father - which is what we all want.

Charity Freeland
Author of *Life Beyond the Scars: Finding Hope in Tragedy*

Dedication

This book is dedicated to those who have an emptiness in their heart due to the absence of a parent. It is hard to fully grasp the depth of the mental and emotional suffering when children and adults experience life without a mom or dad. I know that pain firsthand, and many of you know it as well. Some of you may have had your parents in your life physically but, experienced distant or emotionally absent parents. As you read through these pages, your heart will be squeezed with that familiar ache you vowed to bury. Take heart, friend, and keep reading because what you have longed for is only a few pages away. Some of you have waited your entire life for what is on these pages. You no longer have to earn it, just receive it!

You have longed to hear these words!

To my siblings Donna, Steven, and Monique. I love you for supporting me as I discuss the intimate details of our lives. This writing is not intended to embarrass our family. We have overcome unfortunate circumstances through the grace of God. Now we must share the details of the revelation that has made us whole. Let us share our family secrets so others can heal from emotional wounds, rejection, and loss. They have longed to receive what we now have.

In Loving Memory of Stanley E. Corvin, Jr.

Pop (Stanley E. Corvin Jr.), I will miss your fatherly wisdom. I was able to pick up the phone and say, "I need to talk with the businessman, soldier, family man, Reboot Facilitator, or 12-Step mentor." I loved that our talks always transitioned with me receiving wisdom from my adopted Father. We prayed and dreamed together. Those dreams will not fall to the ground. God will fulfill His purpose through us as you stand among the cloud of witnesses interceding, and we put those prayers into action. There is much work that remains, I am sure you know first-hand these days. Oh, and do not worry, we will take care of "Mom" (Peggy Corvin).

Until we are together again, remember I do not want to do life without you!

I Never Heard My Dad Say
A Journey of Identity and Wholeness

CONTENTS

זִכְּרוֹן

Chapter One

Introduction

As you journey through these pages, understand that this work is being told from my personal experiences. Please don't close the book too soon, thinking, *"I don't relate to this material. He's talking about his dad, but my wounds are from my mother or another family member."* Our experiences might be very different, but how we are healed is the same. A lifetime of pain can be healed. Please, keep reading.

When you visit a doctor because of negative physical or mental symptoms, they begin trying to identify the root cause. After a thorough examination and a series of tests, the doctor presents their conclusion or results. Often, we are perplexed at the root cause. We say things like, *"I would have never imagined that would be the cause."* That is exactly what I said after Jesus revealed the root cause for much of my life's turmoil and, surprisingly, much of my success.

My diagnostic test results arrived. The root cause was losing my dad at a young age. Because of it, I searched for my identity for almost my entire life. During various seasons of my life, I attempted to define myself in various ways. I remember thinking as a young kid, *I will be the toughest gang member. I want to be respected by my homeboys, and feared by those that oppose us.* Thankfully, that phase of my life was not permanent. I was able to rid myself of gang life, but the desire for approval and identity remained. Later in life, I traded my place of identity from gangs to trying to fit in with military life. Everyone looked up to the Special Forces soldiers. "They are the best," I would hear my peers say. I wanted people to look at me and have those same thoughts. Why? Because I was void of my true identity. I craved affirmation. Can you relate to what I am saying?

During the last two years, God has been shining a light in my heart on doors that have been closed. I unknowingly posted "Do Not Enter" signs on them. I did not know those doors existed. I mean, come on, God, I asked Jesus into my heart years ago. How can there be unhealed wounds if I have Jesus living in my heart? When I asked Jesus into my heart, I became a new creation. Everything within me should have instantly been healed, right? Let me explain what happens.

We are made up of three parts: body, soul (mind, will, and emotions), and spirit. The moment you are saved, your spirit comes alive. You go from death to life. Your soul, on the other hand, is a work in progress. This is a word of understanding from what Jesus said, *"The thief does not come except to steal, and to kill, and to destroy. I have come that they may have life and that they may have it more abundantly."*[1] How can Jesus give you life if you are already a living human being? He is referring to your spirit.

After Adam and Eve disobeyed God by eating the forbidden fruit, the life within their spirit died. You can say they became the

---

[1] John 10:10, NKJV

walking dead. In the Scripture above, Jesus gives life to our spirit. From that point, the process of mental and emotional healing starts, which deals with soul wounds. I had a soul wound, and some of you do as well, whether you know it or not. The content of this book will reveal and bring healing to those wounds and to those who have felt orphaned, rejected, or abandoned by a dad or mom.

Thank you for taking this journey toward healing. God is removing those "Do Not Enter" signs on your heart and replacing them with Healed, Whole, and Enter.

דְּרוֹר

Chapter Two

Orphans Rule the World

One Sunday morning in December of 2022, our church had a guest speaker. He caught my attention when he said, "In the book by Os Hillman, *Change Agent: Engaging Your Passion to Be the One Who Makes A Difference*, it was identified that almost three hundred world leaders had been orphans." That blew me away. I had to get that book and read it for myself. If those leaders who had a negative influence on the world could have known the Truth, it would have set them free, and so many others. Fortunately, it is not too late for you and me!

Here is the reference from Os Hillman:

"Dysfunction and abandonment has lifelong consequences in our lives. Recently I came across a little-known fact that demonstrates this dramatically. In a book entitled Creative Suffering, Paul Tournier cites an article written by Dr. Pierre Rentchnick of Geneva, which appeared in a periodical in 1975 under the surprising title "Orphans Lead the World." He went on to explain: "When President Pompidou died, my colleague found himself wondering what might have been the political repercussions of disease in the case of other statesmen, such as for example President Roosevelt at the end of the war. So he set about reading the life-stories of the politicians who had had the greatest influence on the course of world history

[not always positive influence]. He was soon struck by the astonishing discovery that all of them had been orphans!

"Dr. Rentchnick compiled a list of them. It contained almost three hundred of the greatest names in history, from Alexander the Great and Julius Caesar, through Charles V, Cardinal Richelieu, Louis XIV, Robespierre, George Washington, Napoleon, Queen Victoria, Golda Meir, Hitler, Stalin, Lenin, to Eva Peron, Fidel Castro, and Houphouët-Boigny [to name just a few]. All of these leaders suffered in childhood from emotional deprivation. So we are giving lectures on how important it is for a child's development to have a father and a mother performing harmoniously together their respective roles toward him. And all at once we find that this is the very thing that those who have been most influential in world history have not had! From this surprising revelation my colleague deduced 'a new theory of genesis of the will to political power': the insecurity consequent upon emotional deprivation must have aroused in these children an exceptional will to power, which drove them into a career in politics with the aim of 'transforming the world' and succeeding in so far as they were able. Thus an unconscious will to power seems to play an important part in the lives of the most eminent men."[2,3]

Culture truly is shaped positively or negatively by early childhood experiences. These leaders had an imbalance in their souls. Unhealed pain caused by a lack of nurture and a lack of understanding

---

[2] Paul Tournier, *Creative suffering* (New York: Harper and Row Publishers, 1983), 1-2

[3] Os Hillmam, *Change Agent: Engaging Your Passion to Be the One Who Makes A Difference* (Florida: Charisma House Publishers, 2011) 115-116

of who they truly were fed their self-driven will to find a way to set it all straight, to transform the world, and to prove they were worthy, capable beings. They lacked the security that comes from having a healthy, responsible person to protect and guide them. In a desperate attempt to compensate for what they had not had, they attempted to create the world in the image they believed was right.

Mankind has never been able to view the world with a broad understanding of "right" like the one who created it does. Disharmony seen in a world led by individuals striving for power is also found in homes established by emotionally deprived children who have never known their fathers.

Root Cause

Life was pretty normal for me growing up in Whittier, California, in the 1980s and 1990s. At least what I perceived as normal. My normal was living in a home with only one of my biological parents steering the ship. Sometimes that ship spun in circles, and other times veered off course mainly because the captain was absent. Who was the captain of my ship? I am glad you asked. It was my dad.

My dad was introduced to alcohol at a young age. I was told it was his uncles who exposed him to it so they could be amused. They did not introduce him to something that could have been life-giving, like following family traditions in education or being an entrepreneur. Instead, they put a death sentence in his hand. What died at the hands of alcohol? My dad's career, his future, his marriage, and dreams of raising his children, and sadly at 34 years old, he died.

I was approximately five years old when he died. At that age, I did not understand what I had lost. No child is mature enough to understand the depth of losing a dad and the impact it has on their identity. I was lost without him. I recall having questions like, *"I wonder if my dad did it that way. I know that I like doing that, but is it because I am following after my dad?"* Those questions ranged from hobbies, education, family, career selection, and more.

The Bible says we are made in the image and likeness of God. That means my dad should have been a living reflection of the divine likeness of our heavenly Father. Since I didn't have Dad to reflect God's image in my life, I was lost. God's perfect design and plan for my family was altered by my dad's free will and alcohol abuse.

Because of the absence of Godly influence from him in my developmental years, I did not have a relationship with Jesus. I knew of Him, but that knowledge was minimal at best. He was the God we honored, prayed to, and visited on occasions at church. And that is exactly where I left Him, at church. He was the distant relative you see only a couple of times a year.

After my dad passed away, Jesus continued His endless pursuit of us through my grandma Rosie. She had a strong influence on my life but not to the degree a dad has on a child during their formative years. Yet that never stopped Grandma from giving me words of encouragement and calling the prayer line for me. I am alive to write this book because she never wavered in her faithfulness in praying for me. I rejoice in my God, who is faithful to fulfill prayers. Sadly,

Grandma passed away before seeing hers fulfilled. She did not see the realization of what she prayed for my entire life. I am a living testament to the power of prayer over grandchildren. It can never be overstated, do not go off of what you see in the natural or limit God to the timeframe you expect. Please keep praying and believing that God is working all things out for you and what you are praying for.

I know it sounds like this is a pity party, but stick with me; we are getting to the root cause. During those formative years, I did what most orphans do: I tried to create my own identity. I was going to be a man's man. Unfortunately, I did not know how to create an identity. So, my friends became my source of identity and approval.

Wait! A child should receive identity from their dad. He was supposed to *"train me up in the way I should go."*[4] But he was not around. It is not hard to conclude; the train had begun to slide off the tracks heading for disaster.

My new-found sources of approval began to get involved with gangs. I desperately wanted them to think I was the man, so what action did I take? I joined a gang. Did that fill the void in my heart? No way! I did not have time to think about myself and my feelings. I was too busy running for my life from rival gang members. You need to hear this. People pleasing and creating your own identity go hand in hand, and both leave you feeling empty and alone.

I have to add this story. In the two years between my high school graduation and enlisting in the military, I worked various jobs.

---

[4] Paraphrase Proverbs 22:6

One of those was delivering meat for an independent small business. There were only a handful of us working for Mr. Phil. My workday started at 7 a.m., but I usually cut it close, and often I was flat-out late. Mr. Phil needed me out on my route as soon as I was loaded because the restaurants needed their supplies. If there was a large amount to deliver or I ran late, he would help me load the delivery van. Without realizing it, I began to open my heart to Mr. Phil. He didn't realize it either. I wanted that fatherly relationship I never experienced with my dad. It was almost like a dad taking his son to the park and tossing the football. I looked forward to loading the van with him.

One day I walked into his office and said, *"You want to load the van with me?"* What my heart was really saying was, *"I want dad time with you."* He looked at me and said, *"That is why I pay you."* Talk about a shotgun blast to the heart. It took everything within me not to cry in his office. It was not his fault. He did not know what was happening in my heart. Sadly, neither did I. I hope you dads, who are reading this, will be careful how you respond to your kids. Your words have a lasting impact and hurt more than sticks and stones. I never asked him again to load the van with me. I left his business with that emptiness persisting in my heart.

Until addressed, you will carry the symptoms from an orphaned heart with you. They show themselves differently in a child as opposed to an adult. As I mentioned, during my formative years, my sources of identity and approval were my knuckle-headed friends. I later joined the military needing discipline and a way to put my life in order. Guess what I was still searching for? Identity.

I was first assigned to the US Army's 82nd Airborne Division, Fort Bragg, NC. My first unit became the foundation for the remainder of my 20-year career. I was taught by great leaders to work hard, perform with excellence, be a self-starter, and to never quit. These were traits I should have learned from my dad. Children need parents in their lives who reflect Christ simply through the way they live. There is a tremendous void in the hearts of children when their parents are absent or distant, and there is a distinct longing to fill the void.

Even in my new setting, it did not take long before that familiar longing resurfaced. That orphan heart that craved affirmation remained; this time, it was masked in a camouflage uniform and esprit de corps. For those that believe *"I will change my friends or my location, and that will change me or my situation."* Wrong! You have to seek God and ask Him to help you identify the root cause behind your behavior, addiction, broken heart, or anything keeping you from knowing who He created you to be.

Since Fort Bragg is home to the Army's Special Operations, seeing Green Berets and Rangers on base was normal. Everyone knew they were the elite warfighters. Soldiers stepped out of the way if a Green Beret was on their walking path. I eventually became a Green Beret. It was a monumental achievement. One that not many achieve, even those who are smarter, faster, and stronger than me.

In 2022, God revealed my true motive for wanting to be a Green Beret. Yes, I wanted to be an elite soldier, but there was something else within me that was my true motivation. It was my root cause. I craved affirmation! Since everyone saw the Green Berets as the best, I wanted them to think the same about me. Why did I have this unhealthy craving? Because I lacked affirmation from my dad. I never heard my dad say, *"You are my son in whom I am well pleased. You are my son; I love you."* Why has it taken until I was 44 years old to receive this revelation? Because revelation is only received through a relationship with Jesus. The world is a treasure trove of information, just waiting to be discovered by those who seek it. Yet, information will never substitute revelation.

Does this resonate with you? Have you struggled wondering why you feel sad or need approval from others? Stay with me till the end. Your healing is only a few pages away!

דרור

Chapter Three

What the Heart is Really Saying

Something happened during a recent event that hit me in my heart. I am using personal experiences from my life because I see how God is changing me, and I hope my experiences will help you see God even more clearly, too. Those experiences range from good and joyful to heartbreak and sadness. Well, here I go sharing intimate details of my life in hopes you will learn from my mishaps.

Since I'm a minister, you would think I have it all figured out and do not make relational mistakes. Wrong! I need the grace Jesus offers today as much as I did years ago when my life spiraled out of control. Hopefully, we are all lifelong learners. I need to hurry and publish this book before God uses something else from my life to add another chapter.

I recently visited my family in California. One of my sons lives there with his wife and son, and my mother and siblings are not far from him. It is always a great time going home, but it can quickly get busy when we are trying to add visits with family and friends. My main goal is always to give my son, who is my first priority, my full attention. Sadly, I have failed to hit the mark at times. Thank goodness God gives us grace and opportunities to learn and correct those mistakes.

This visit was hectic because I spoke at CityReach Church in my hometown of Whittier, California. I invited family and friends, hoping to share Jesus with them. To my surprise, several family members attended. Even better, my son, his lovely wife, and my grandson were in attendance. When they walked in, my heart said, *Thank you, Lord, for redeeming my legacy.* The service was powerful, but it was an announcement to everyone that I was home.

Please do not take what I am saying the wrong way. We love visiting with our family and friends; however, that brought some challenges. My son has contended with my military service and my living out of state nearly his entire life. Since he was young, we would only get to visit together once or maybe twice a year. Take a week-long visit and divide the time between family, friends, and my son; how much quality time did he get? Truthfully, not as much as he wanted nor as much as I had hoped to give. A few hours a year of face-to-face time will never be enough for anyone who needs and desires time with their dad or mom.

These days, getting quality time with my son is a bit more challenging since he has his own family and responsibilities. So, during my visit, I tried scheduling family and friend visits when he was occupied with his family. He appeared happy while we were together, so I assumed everything was fine. Never assume anything because the reality is usually the opposite. After a week and a half, our visit was wrapping up. I was a bit tired from visiting with everyone, but overall, I felt good about it. Then my assumption was discredited when my son dropped the truth straight from his heart.

As he spoke, the truth pierced right through my heart because

I knew he was right. *"Dad, I don't feel like we got quality time together."* My heart broke because how many times in his life had he felt that way but never told me? I wondered how often his heart ached as I waved goodbye at the airport. Because we had driven, Angel and I could extend our trip and give him the attention he had longed for his entire life. I am sure many of you can relate to my son's heart cry.

My son competed for my attention almost his entire life. Part of the reason for my not being fully present was that I was proudly serving the US military. I let that become an excuse for not giving him my full attention. If you have a similar situation or a demanding job, don't allow anything to be a reason for not fully investing in your kids. Become aware of making every minute count with your children.

Many people live with their children and are absent parents. Please wake up to the fact that your family needs you to be present and sober. You might say, *"I work long hours to provide for them. That justifies my absence."* They appreciate your hard work, but material items will never substitute for your attention. Sticking a smartphone, tablet, game system, or TV in their face to keep them occupied is not parenting. Don't be unaware that it only breeds orphans when you are not present and engaged with them.

The heart cries my son expressed are no different from the ones I carried for years. Fortunately for him, I am alive to correct my mishaps and be the daddy God called me to be. The truth is there is no age limit on those tears. Many of you are still longing for attention from your dad or mom. Regardless of your age, if your parent(s) is alive, be bold like my son was with me and speak up.

Tell them you desire their time. Maybe they are like me and grew up without a dad or mom, so they need help in areas that do not come naturally. Extend grace and forgiveness to your dad or mom. Don't let their failings keep you from being the very best child you can be. Do not be afraid to start the process of healing the void in your heart. It might take time, but at least there is motion. Jesus' anointing brings healing to broken hearts. You have carried this brokenness long enough. His presence in your life gives you the strength to deal with the tough stuff and find restoration for your soul.

Sometimes we have to grow up and become a daddy or mommy before we can see our parents differently. One morning as I started my time with the Lord in prayer, I had a memory of my dad from long ago that caused me to understand more about him. I remembered my brother riding his bicycle in the street in front of our house. My dad flew out of the house and yelled at my brother, "Get out of the street." As kids, all we understood was that our dad was very strict. Sometimes it caused us to think that meant he didn't love us. As I sat with that memory, all of a sudden, another time flashed into my mind.

My brother had a 10-speed bike that he rode all the time. We followed a regular course around the neighborhood. One day, that loop around the neighborhood changed his life. He was headed toward his friend's house, but as he made the last turn, he was hit by a car. The collision was so loud that neighbors heard it and came to help. One of the 10-speed pedals gouged into my brother's shin, exposing the bone.

I remember frantic knocks from a neighbor who tried to reach my mom and Grandma to tell them about the accident. It was all very scary. My Mom spent the next several days with my brother at the hospital. During that time, my dad would pick me up and take care of me. I remember he took me to McDonald's on the way to the hospital to visit my brother. It was a special time between my dad and me; a time when I felt he cared.

As a dad myself, I now understand how frightened my dad was when a car hit my brother. It made him realize how much he cared about his kids. Shortly after that accident, he started yelling at us when we did anything he thought would put us in danger.

He didn't have the emotional ability to sit us all down and explain his feelings. He couldn't tell us how much he loved us. He couldn't say how scared he felt when he thought something bad might happen to us. The fact that he couldn't say it didn't mean he didn't feel the love and desire to protect and take care of us. He couldn't offer us something he didn't have to give. Remembering he was hurt by being given alcohol at a very early age caused a new revelation in me. I was a wounded child of a wounded child.

Until Jesus started transforming my life, I had acted the only way I knew, out of the unhealed wounds in my heart. I know I hurt my children by operating out of fear. I didn't have a clue how to be a dad and felt inadequate until the Father said, *Get Up, John!* and set me on a different path. His rhema word stirred my soul and awoke my Spirit.

Having this memory of my dad was like returning to the

location where I had been shot thirty days earlier. Going back to Ft. Hood that day, I claimed my victory over fear. But in my prayer room, remembering my dad that morning, I stood up and declared that I would learn from my dad and stop being a wounded father of a wounded father. When I feel fear about my children, I now know that I must express what my heart is saying. Not my emotions. God made me a dad for our children. God will transform me to be the dad He created me to be. He is the only one who can teach me how to do it right.

I'm committed to letting Holy Spirit lead me and teach me what being a dad is like. I still get caught up in the old responses, however. They are imprinted in my brain. But now, I see why I am doing those old things, and Holy Spirit prompts my heart to do it differently.

Recently an issue arose in my relationship with another son. I feel some lifestyle choices he is making are very harmful. He is a grown man, so I respect his right to make his own choices; however, I won't participate with him in those choices or enable him to keep making them. I thought the boundaries were very clear, but then something happened that made me think he had crossed the line.

I consistently pray for his strength to make different choices and gain victory. I trust God to help him, but somewhere in my "dad's heart" lies the fear that comes from feeling he may not let God. When he crossed the line, my old knee-jerk response of *"fear turned to anger"* flew out of me. I said some biting words that were far sharper than they needed to be. I ended our conversation abruptly because of the direction it was going.

Of course, Holy Spirit was not happy with that outburst and didn't let me stay comfortable with it. I have come to understand that Holy Spirit isn't an enabler either! After much prayer, God's peace flooded my heart and empowered me to reach out to my son with love. These were my next words, *"I know my words can come across as sounding mean. It's my heart that's broken for you. I just want you free! I hate watching you live like this. I can say a lot of things to you but don't ever think that I stopped loving you. Parents have to set rules with their children but it's from the love in their heart. Yes, I am upset with you. But that does not mean I don't love you. Don't ever believe a lie like that."*

The Apostle Paul has great instructions for fathers, *"Fathers, do not provoke your children to anger by the way you treat them. Rather, bring them up with the discipline and instruction that comes from the Lord."*[5] If we didn't have the ways of the Lord to give to our kids when they were young, we might feel it is too late to change things now. Feelings are not the truth. It is never too late. Holy Spirit reminded me that I was a fully grown man the day My Father instructed me to *"Get Up!"* Amazingly, He hasn't stopped giving me instructions since. God, our Father, never stops pursuing us as His children, regardless of our age. We are never too old for Him to coach us on how to be loving parents, no matter how we started.

My dad loved me with all the love he had, and he expressed it

---

[5] Ephesians 6:4, NLT

in the only ways he knew. My constant prayer is that Holy Spirit will teach me and you the right ways to love with all this love He has poured into our hearts. I also often ask that we learn to tame our tongues to express what our heart is saying.

דְּרוֹר

Chapter Four

Long Suffering

I was praying for God to remove a family member's desire for alcohol. My prayers were out of frustration. My heart was making statements like, *"Okay, God, if they won't, then I am asking You to..."* You fill in the blanks because we have all been there. By the way, this was not years ago; it was days ago.

I prayed that the fruit of the Spirit would manifest in my family. The fruit of the Spirit is what we see grow in our lives when we are filled with the Spirit and awareness of God's presence in us. Galatians chapter 5 lists what we will see.

"But the fruit of the Spirit is love, joy, peace, **_longsuffering_**_, kindness, goodness, faithfulness, gentleness, self-control. Against such there is no law."_

I keyed in on the word longsuffering. It would not leave my thoughts. It was almost how you see it on this page -- bold and underlined. I began to talk with God about it, asking Him what He was trying to show me. Before I proceed, let me share several words synonymous with longsuffering so you understand the meaning. Longsuffering can be substituted with words like tolerant, accommodating, and patient. What was God revealing? For me to be patient with this family member.

We forget how patient God has been with us. He didn't

transform us in one split second. He walked with us, leading us to understand His ways. Our frustration sets in towards others when we want immediate, complete transformation in their life. When we don't see that, we may even think, God, remove them from my life. I'm sure some of you are thinking, John, you don't make statements like that, right? Wrong! Those were my words. Harsh. Yeah, I know, which is why our loving Father asked me to take on His character by being patient.

I know many people who think, *John, I hear you, but when has God been longsuffering? Isn't He waiting for us to mess up so that He can punish us?* Understanding what is recorded about the journey to the promised land reveals His longsuffering. God selected land for the Israelites to possess. He was excited for His people to inherit such prime real estate. He told them their land flowed with milk and honey. They were coming out of 400 years of slavery in Egypt. Moses was their leader then, and God met with Him face-to-face. They were set to cross the Jordan River and possess their inheritance.

In the thirteenth and fourteenth chapters of the Book of Numbers, the Bible tells us they spied out the land because it was inhabited, and they would have to remove the squatters. Moses sent 12 spies who surveyed the land for 40 days. They returned carrying produce from the land that was so large it required two men to carry. The land was exactly as God said it would be, flowing with abundance.

The problem was that 10 of the 12 spies gave a bad report. *"There are giants in the land, and we are like grasshoppers in their sight. We will be slaughtered, there is no way we will overcome the giants. "* [6] Only 2 of the 12 spies possessed enough faith to trust God for victory over the inhabitants of the promised land. Unfortunately, the people sided with the ten men who rebelled and caused unbelief. The Israelites returned to the desert for 40 years before finally possessing their inheritance.

Here is the moral of the story. Did the Israelites rebel against God? Yes. Did they have to return to the desert because of their rebellion and unbelief? Yes. Did God abandon them in the desert and find Himself a new group of people who would trust and believe in Him? No! Did God move to His Plan B because His Plan A failed? NO!

He is long-suffering! He returned to the desert with them. Even in their rebellion, He would not leave them. Listen to the words of Moses in the book of Deuteronomy as he is reminding the Israelites about that: *"And I have led you forty years in the wilderness. Your clothes have not worn out on you, and your sandals have not worn out on your feet. "*[7] God's love for us is so great that He never leaves us! Not even when things in our lives are not pleasing to Him. He is telling us to do the same towards others. Formulating a Plan B or asking God to remove someone because their freedom is taking too long is easy. God is asking you to be patient and, if need be, return to the desert with them.

The same day God talked to me about longsuffering, I had a

---

[6] Numbers 13:33, NKJV
[7] Deuteronomy 29: 5, NKJV

conversation with a friend. This friend and I are pretty close, and we hold nothing back. We have some deep conversations. He began sharing about his childhood. Overall, he had a good childhood and was raised in a loving home. Yet, a few situations in that home flipped a switch on the inside of him and put up walls designed to protect his heart.

He said, *"At a young age, I determined I had to take care of myself."* What was pouring from his heart was that he had a large family. He felt insignificant in a sea of siblings. He felt unseen and unloved. My friend didn't realize that he carried those wounds into his marriage. Is he a good man who loves and gives? Yes, he is. However, his wife has had to chisel through the fortified walls around his heart. You do know that those barriers you set up as a child do not remove themselves, right? If they are not removed, you carry them while building your own family. When that happens, the people you love most must deal with them.

My friend had several recent revelations about how much his wife actually loved him. He teared up as he spoke. The truth is, he had walls up so high around his heart it was hard for him to see her acts of love. As he continued, I began to picture a movie scene in my mind. It was my friend walking through the Grand Canyon. He was walking as if he was guiding a tour, but there was only one follower. It was his wife. She had been following the entire time. Her longsuffering for him had her trailing him in the desert for years. He didn't realize it because of the fortified walls he set up around his heart as a child. I am happy to share that there has been transformation in their marriage.

They are walking out of the desert side-by-side, holding hands.

When barriers are set up in our hearts, we think they only affect areas and people they are intended to keep out. Wrong! Think about traffic barriers or road closed signs. Does the barrier understand that cars are prohibited, but bicycles are allowed? No. It takes a traffic attendant to supervise the construction to apply the intended desire. We set up barriers in our hearts and then forget they are there until they begin to affect our lives and relationships. Guess who else is affected by our barriers? God.

I'm sure some of you are thinking, John, I would never put up a barrier between me and God. You don't intend to, but when you set up barriers for others, then He is not allowed in either. To make matters worse, over time, we forget the walls are in place. Without Him, the barriers can never be removed, and there can be no healing. Like with the Israelites, He is forced to enter the desert yet again until we let Him in.

Proverbs 4:23 is often misunderstood, *"Guard your heart above all else, for it determines the course of your life."* This doesn't mean to keep people out by closing your heart. The Hebrew word that is translated as "guard" actually means "watch over, as you would watch over a vineyard." Plant good things, watch over it to see it is nourished, water it, feed it, and stamp out any pestilence. Pause for a minute to hear and reflect on what "feeds your heart." What brings you joy and peace? Most of us will say "love."

If you know you have heart wounds that have not been healed, don't suffer in the barren wasteland of an isolated, loveless life. Pray to Him. If you don't know how, tell Him you don't know how. Ask Him to help you and to give you the courage to bring this to Him. Here is a sample prayer that is being prayed over people who are reading this book. We wrote this for you!

Lord, I admit that there is layer after layer of pain in my heart. I have not brought it to You, and I have let it fester until my heart has become hard toward You and other people. Sometimes, God, I feel like you could have stopped what happened to me, and you didn't. Lord, I am sorry that I have hurt you and others because of the pain in my heart. Forgive me, Lord. I don't know how to do this differently, but I am willing to learn from You. I am setting aside my fear, my hurt, the anger I feel toward others, and the belief that I can be in charge of all this. I give it all to You. I am asking now for Your Holy Spirit to come in and fill me up. Light up the dark places, speak your Truth over all the lies, save me from this desert way of life, Lord. I want You and Your will for my life, nothing else. AMEN!

Rest in God's presence. Listen for His voice. Before you press on to the rest of this chapter, take as much time as needed to pray and allow the Holy Spirit to saturate your soul.

It is important to notice how the verses in Galatians are written. In this use, the Greek word for fruit means the work or the result of something. With that in mind, we can know that it doesn't just happen. It is the work of the Spirit. It is the result of letting Holy Spirit lead us. The Bible is very intentional. Nothing is meaningless. There is an order to the list of fruit.

"But the fruit of the Spirit [the result of His presence within us] is love [unselfish concern for others], joy [not fleeting happiness], peace [inner shalom], patience [not the ability to wait, but how we act while waiting], kindness [meeting real needs, in God's way, in His timing] goodness [goodness that comes from God, showing itself in spiritual, moral excellence] faithfulness [unfailingly loyal], gentleness [power with reserve and gentleness], and self-control [dominion within but not by oneself; it only comes from Spirit]."[8]

All you grammarians probably noticed that the subject (fruit) is paired with a singular verb (is), yet the subject is not singular. If stated in reverse order, it would be, "Love, joy, peace, patience, kindness, goodness, faithfulness, gentleness, and self-control are the fruits of the Spirit."

The Bible does not contain errors. The fruit is love. All the other attributes are absolutely impossible to have without love. Love is the basis for Kingdom living. Our character and our quality of life are dependent on Love.

The Apostle Paul explained it another way, "If I could speak all the languages of earth and of angels, but didn't love others, I would only be a noisy gong or a clanging cymbal. If I had the gift of prophecy, and if I understood all of God's secret plans and possessed all knowledge, and if I had such faith that I could move mountains, but didn't love others, I would be nothing. If I gave everything I have to the poor and even sacrificed my body, I could boast about it; but if

---

[8] Galatians 5:22-23, AMP

I didn't love others, I would have gained nothing."[9]

Everything it takes to make our lives and relationships work begins with True Love that only comes from God's presence within us. When He comes to us, He wants to send His Spirit into us to show us how much He loves us. Until we know that deep inside our hearts, we will never be willing to break down the barriers we think will protect us.

The amount of joy, peace, patience, kindness, goodness, faithfulness, gentleness, and self-control that we have in our life is in direct proportion to the amount of Love that we let His Spirit flow into us. By opening up to receive His love, we will have something of great value to pour into the people around us.

If you have a person in your life who is upsetting you right now, the first thing you should do is pray. No, not for the other person. You should be on your knees, thanking God for trusting you enough to place a wounded, hurting person on your path. He believes *you* may be the one that will let Him love them enough through you that they can come to know Him, too. He wants to redeem them, just like He did with you.

Momentary aggravation over what another person is doing is a small price to pay to partner with their Creator and see one of God's most treasured possessions restored to Him. It cost Jesus a whole lot more than that to save each one of us!

---

[9] 1 Corinthians 13:1-3, NLT

דוֹרוֹ

Chapter *Five*

The Truth

This chapter is the reason for writing this book. For you, this is where the pain caused by lies ends, and truth takes root. *"All right, John, give us the truth!"* Not yet, you remember what mom said, "Dessert after dinner."

Many of you have heard of the biblical character David. As children, we were taught about his triumphant victory. Most of us know how this young shepherd boy defeated the giant Goliath of the Philistine army with only a sling and a stone. Amazingly, the victory happened while valiant men, King Saul, the king of Israel, and David's own brothers cowered in fear because of Goliath. This creates a thought in my heart. Lord, I believe countless men, women, and children reading this book will receive the truth about their identity. They are the Davids of our generation. They will run at the giants of our time with spiritual weapons defeating them with Your word as others look on from the sidelines.

Back to David. He is first mentioned in 1 Samuel 16 when he was anointed by the Prophet Samuel to become the second king of Israel after capturing God's heart. There is an important truth you need to understand about David. God did not preselect David to one day become king before anointing Saul so that Saul would merely be an interim king until David was ready. No. King Saul was God's chosen man from the beginning, but his disobedience caused God to remove His Spirit from him and search for a replacement. David was God's replacement for a disobedient chosen king. What does that say about you and me? Do not force God to find an alternate for you!

"And Samuel said, "What have you done?"

Saul said, "When I saw that the people were scattered from me, and that you did not come within the days appointed, and that the Philistines gathered together at Michmash, then I said, 'The Philistines will now come down on me at Gilgal, and I have not made supplication to the Lord.' Therefore I felt compelled, and offered a burnt offering."

And Samuel said to Saul, "You have done foolishly. You have not kept the commandment of the Lord your God, which He commanded you. For now the Lord would have established your kingdom over Israel forever. But now your kingdom shall not continue. The Lord has sought for Himself a man after His own heart, and the Lord has commanded him to be commander over His people, because you have not kept what the Lord commanded you."[10]

The Bible chronicles David's life, first as a boy, then later as a man of war then ultimately as king of Israel. David was not perfect. He made mistakes, but that just made him even more dependent on God. Read through the book of Psalms, and you will quickly get a glimpse into his journey from shepherd boy to king. You will see a true understanding of his relationship and dependence on God. This is

---

[10] Replacing Saul, 1 Samuel 13:11-14, NKJV

important for you to understand; David's character made room for his anointing and assignment. What do I mean? Before David was appointed king of Israel, he went through a great deal of adversity. God used his trials to develop his character. It has been that way in my life, too. God did not shoot me, but He used the circumstances for my good.

Without established character, our reign will be short-lived. If God had positioned David as king the moment he was anointed, he would have failed. At that point in his life, his relationship with God was strong, but his character was inadequate for his calling. As king, he had a moral failure, yet his proven character and yielded heart caused him to repent. It's important to note that when he failed morally, he did not approach God like many others would have.

Those without character say, *"God, do not take away my kingdom, status, influence, or riches."* It would be all about them. Observe David's prayer, as recorded in Psalms 51:11 *"Do not cast me away from Your presence, And do not take Your Holy Spirit from me."* When sin has you in its clutches and begins to squeeze, the real you will come out. Inside David was a man after God's heart with character forged in the secret place of God's presence. Unfortunately, it took a bit of a squeeze for David to get back on course.

I expounded on David's character for a reason. It revealed how David could honor his covenant with his best friend, Jonathan, King Saul's son. The Bible explains that David and Jonathan formed a *bond greater than just a casual friendship.*[11] Their covenant saved David's life through Jonathan and later restored Jonathan's son, Mephibosheth, to his royal lineage through David.

The Bible describes David's turmoil as King Saul sought to kill him.

"King Saul was jealous of him and knew that the Lord was with David. Yet, Jonathan did not share his father's resentment towards David but instead loved him as he loved himself. Jonathan knew the Lord was with David and that David was God's chosen king of Israel. Jonathan helped David escape and avoid being killed by King Saul, but before they parted ways, Jonathan had David promise that he would not destroy his household when he became king. In fact, at a later encounter with David, Jonathan said, "The hand of my father Saul will not find you. You will be king over Israel and I will be second in command to you; my father Saul knows this too." [12]

That is a bold statement. It would have to be a true love for one another for that to be fulfilled. The custom was that those newly crowned kings removed any potential opponents. The former king's household was where they started. Unfortunately, Jonathan was never able to see his declaration come to pass. King Saul's disobedience not only impacted him but his sons as well. Scripture tells us that King Saul and his son Jonathan lost their lives in a battle against the Philistines.[13] At this point, David's character and his covenant with

---

[11] See 1 Samuel 20-23
[12] 1 Samuel 23:17, AMP
[13] In 1 Samuel 31

Jonathan intersect.

God is intentional about the words included in the Scriptures. The story of Mephibosheth, Jonathan's son, was included to guide us all to find our true identity. The Bible describes in 2 Samuel 4: 4 (AMP) *"Jonathan, Saul's son, had a son whose feet were crippled. He was five years old when the news [of the deaths] of Saul and Jonathan came from Jezreel. And the boy's nurse picked him up and fled; but it happened that while she was hurrying to flee, he fell and became lame. His name was Mephibosheth."*

The nurse fled, fearing that the incoming king would kill everyone from King Saul's household. Where did Mephibosheth end up? Lo-debar. The Hebrew word for Lo-debar means *"no pasture or pasture less."* In one day, Mephibosheth went from being a prince's son, where he might have inevitably become king in Israel, to being orphaned with no daddy and living in a wilderness crippled in his feet.

Wow! Think about the contrast of his life from one day to the next. Are there Mephibosheth's reading this book? Have you been through tragedy or trauma that has impacted you emotionally, physically, and financially? If so, you might be a resident of Lo-debar, the wilderness. Do not lose heart, my friend, freedom is here. Keep reading.

The next time Mephibosheth is mentioned, David's character is once again on display.

"And David said, "Is there still anyone left of the house (family) of Saul to whom I may show kindness for Jonathan's sake?" There was a servant of the house of Saul whose name was Ziba, so

they called him to David. And the king said to him, "Are you Ziba?"
He said, "I am your servant." And the king said, "Is there no longer
anyone left of the house (family) of Saul to whom I may show the
goodness and graciousness of God?"

Ziba replied to the king, "There is still a son of Jonathan,
[one] whose feet are crippled." So the king said to him, "Where is
he?" And Ziba replied to the king, "He is in the house of Machir the
son of Ammiel, in Lo-debar." Then King David sent word and had
him brought from the house of Machir the son of Ammiel, from Lo-
debar.

Mephibosheth the son of Jonathan, the son of Saul, came to
David and fell face down and lay himself down [in respect]. David
said, "Mephibosheth." And he answered, "Here is your
servant!" David said to him, "Do not be afraid, for I will certainly
show you kindness for the sake of your father Jonathan, and will
restore to you all the land of your grandfather Saul; and you shall
always eat at my table."

Again Mephibosheth lay himself face down and said, "What is
your servant, that you would be concerned for a dead dog like me?"
Then the king summoned Ziba, Saul's servant, and said to him, "I have
given your master's grandson everything that belonged to Saul and to
all his house (family). You and your sons and your servants shall
cultivate the land for him, and you shall bring in the produce, so that
your master's grandson may have food to eat; but Mephibosheth, your
master's grandson, shall always eat at my table." Now Ziba had
fifteen sons and twenty servants. Then Ziba said to the king, "Your
servant will do according to everything that my lord the king
commands." So Mephibosheth ate at David's table as one of the
king's sons. Mephibosheth had a young son whose name was Mica.
And all who lived in Ziba's house were servants to Mephibosheth. So

Mephibosheth lived in Jerusalem, for he always ate at the king's table. And he was lame in both feet.[14]

It is important that I include that entire chapter. This book is rooted in what God revealed in that chapter. Think about this, Mephibosheth went from the palace to the wilderness in one day and ultimately spent a good part of his life in the wilderness even though he was royalty. Then his greatest fear became a reality, his location was revealed to the king, and he was summoned. I am sure he assumed, *"My life is over. Today I will be reunited with my father, Jonathan."* Do you remember I said, "When sin squeezes, what is inside you will come out?" The pressure of the situation put a squeeze on him, and how Mephibosheth saw himself came out before the king. *"Again Mephibosheth lay himself face down and said, **"What is your servant, that you would be concerned for a dead dog like me?"***[15]

Wow! He saw himself as a dead dog. He not only lived in Lo-debar, Lo-debar lived in him! In that encounter with King David, Mephibosheth regained his family's land and was restored to what had belonged to him all along, a seat at the king's table. In one day, he lost everything, and in one day, everything was restored to him.

Are you asking, *"Where is he going with this?"* This chapter is not about David, Jonathan, or Mephibosheth. **It is about you.** When you look in the mirror, do you see Mephibosheth? Do you see yourself as a dead dog? Do you live in your own emotional Lo-debar? Did you grow up without a dad or mom? Maybe your parents divorced, and

---

[14] 2 Samuel 9, AMP
[15] 2 Samuel 9:8, AMP

everything changed instantly, and you went from the palace to the wilderness. Maybe like me, you were never affirmed by your dad. You never heard *"I am proud of you. You are my child in whom I am well pleased."* Maybe your efforts were never good enough for your family. Did you go searching for love and significance only to find brokenness? Have you chased "Likes" on social media as your source for affirmation?

You no longer have to chase "Likes" because you, my friend, are loved! You need to know that you have been deceived. Yes. You believed a lie. You might not have lived with a dad in your life or heard those endearing words, *"I love you. I am proud of you."* The truth is, you have always had a Father that loves and adores you. His name is God, and He sent His Son Jesus to earth for the greatest hostage rescue mission ever executed. He sent Jesus for you! God knows everything about you. He has been with you every time you cried. He showed up at every game and recital. He smiled as you took prom photos. He was at your graduation. And guess what? He is not angry with you. He is not waiting for you to make a mistake so He can punish you. He is a good Father. While you were in your mother's womb, God knew you and named you. It says it in His word. *"Listen to Me, O islands and coastlands, And pay attention, you peoples from far away.* ***The Lord has called Me from the womb; From the body of My mother He has named Me."*** [16]

Who has the privilege of naming children? Parents. Like

---

[16] Isaiah 49:1, AMP

Mephibosheth, you are royalty. You have always been royalty. Jesus' blood flows through your veins. Consider this, a convoy of limousines arrives at your home. Men and women, all dressed professionally with security all around, knock at your door. They have evidence that you were born into the royal lineage, and the King sends them to invite you to dine at the king's table for the rest of your life. How would you respond? You would get up, pull your shoulders back, lift your head, and shed the dead dog identity.

Scripture relates a very important incident that happened in Jesus' life on earth. *When all the people were baptized, it came to pass that Jesus also was baptized; and while He prayed, the heaven was opened. And the Holy Spirit descended in bodily form like a dove upon Him, and a voice came from Heaven which said, **"You are My beloved Son; in You I am well pleased."*** [17] At that point in Jesus' life, His ministry had not yet started. He had not preached one message nor healed anyone. Yet, His Father was already proud of Him. Jesus never had to earn His Father's love; He simply had to receive it. Do you realize you have the same Father Jesus has? You are His beloved son or daughter, too. Friend, you do not have to earn your Father's love. You just receive it. It has always been yours.

I have been sent to escort you to the King's table. Your Father is the King of Kings. Now it is time that you understand and walk in your real identity.

---

[17] Luke 3: 21-22, NKJV

The King Requests
The Pleasure of Your Company
At His Table

Please R.S.V.P.

You have heard some of my compelling reasons for writing this book. When I responded to God's voice when He told me to "Get Up!" He set me on a journey that led to a close, personal relationship with Him. I have experienced amazing moments with Him, creating a passionate desire in me to work alongside Him to *"set the captives free."*[18] I have met many people who share a heart passion similar to mine to see believers get free to be fully who they were created to be. One of those people, Peggy Corvin, and I are working together to create this book to use as a freedom tool.

As co-author, she has added the following section to address ways to identify and defeat the strongholds of lies, labels, and limitations that traumatic and negative events have put into our lives. As Freedom Minister, she has diligently brought the cry for true freedom to believers for years.

She was born into abject poverty and suffered every type of abuse a child can experience for the first five years of her life. She was taken from that situation and adopted; however, her new mother had dual addictions to alcohol and rage. Her home was filled with emotional and physical abuse. Brokenness followed her into

---

[18] From Luke 4:18

adulthood, where, at the end of all hope, she was emotionally finished with life. Out of frustration, she yelled at a God she had never known to tell her Why she had ever been born. As she paused before she ended the mistake she was sure this unknown God had made, the first Freedom Minister who ever walked the Earth came to her and brought His Light into her dark world. In His Light, she found who she was all along.

These chapters give insight and explanation about soul wounds to shed light and understanding on the dark shadows from past experiences. The content comes from Holy Spirit's work in her heart as she sought His Presence, spent time in prayer with Him, and continually read and studied His written Word.

This section is intended to engage your heart with His. Read it prayerfully. Ask the Lord to help you deal with the shadows of your past so that you can move into a future filled with the brightness of God's love.

The next chapter tells of each of our journeys with Holy Spirit, from our salvation to transformation. Consider this section the transportation to get you out of Lo-debar by using His ways to get the Lo-debar out of you.

The table is set, and the feast of all manner of good things is ready for you. Will you make your reservation to come, spend time, open up your heart, and claim your royal heritage?

זְרוֹ

Chapter *Six*

Revelations From Our Journey

This chapter is particular. Peggy Corvin and I, collectively, share revelations from our freedom journey. Our journeys will help you understand and apply the follow-on chapters.

Early in your reading, my root cause was revealed. It was an unhealthy craving for approval. I sometimes put it in terms our Western culture recognizes. Chasing likes. Someone posts a story or a selfie on their social media page, hoping someone will affirm them by clicking "Like." Not everyone uses social media for approval, but there are more than you know. Seeking approval has no age limit. Some grandparents were never affirmed and still have heart wounds from their parents. Have you ever wondered why your senior citizen neighbor is always mean and angry? It could be that they have unhealed wounds in their heart. As a gift, give them a copy of this book. They will thank you for it. Joking aside, I carried a lot of baggage that had become part of my everyday journey. Just to name a few, desiring approval, people pleasing, the fear of man, and a failure mentality. These were symptoms of roots that needed to be dug up.

What did you think after reading The Truth? That chapter hopefully was life-transforming. For those who have asked Jesus to reside in their heart, He has given them life. He did it by providing vitality to their spirit. We talked about it earlier. Once Jesus is alive in your heart, you are a child of God. You are royalty and will never again be without a Father fully invested in you. God loves us like we are an only child and heir to His legacy. Think about that. Someone who is an only child will inherit everything that belongs to their parents. God has enough love for us all, making us all His number one's. You don't have to wait until heaven to receive your inheritance.

He wants to save you, heal you, set you free, transform you, and anoint you today. People say, *"I'll be in paradise when I get to heaven. I'll finally be free to live and be loved."* Heaven will be beautiful, no doubt. You don't have to wait; you can experience heaven on earth. I'm not saying wars, famine, and bad things will end, but you can be FREE from the effects of your environment. That's the journey we want to share with you. Your journey begins at the end of this book. Your freedom journey will one day help your spouse, parents, children, friends, and the mean old guy next door.

My freedom journey began years after I was shot at Fort Hood military base in Texas. God showed me that things had not been healed in my heart. I didn't easily fall into His arms and say, "Yes, Jesus, help me clean out the wounds from my past." At first, I thought, "Jesus, how can there be stuff in my heart that needs to be healed or cleaned out? I said the prayer. You know, Jesus! In the salvation prayer, I asked You to be the Lord of my life and dwell in my heart. Jesus, wasn't that a one-and-done prayer, taking care of all the wounds, addictions, and fears from my past?" No. Inviting Jesus into my heart was only the beginning of restoring my spirit, soul, and body. Then what was Jesus wanting to show me that I didn't already know myself? I lived with unhealthy fears and beliefs that became part of my everyday life without ever considering I could be free from them.

Here is an example to help you understand that we can physically be delivered or removed from a bad situation but still be bound in our souls. I got a gang tattoo while serving in the military. I know it's hard to believe, but it's true. Who would do that? Me, and many others that cling to their personal Lo-debar. It is hard to believe, but it's true. God delivered the Israelites from Egypt, where they were in bondage and slavery. Then, the real work began when He had to get Egypt out of them. I'll put it another way. You can take the boy out of the hood (gangs, street life), but you can't take the hood out of the boy. Now I understand why I was still getting gang tattoos early in my military career. My outside environment changed, along with my job and clothes. Inside of me, I was still very much back home.

One day, while in the final phase of the Green Beret qualification course, my team walked to the chow hall. I saw a friend that was on another team. I yelled out, "What's up, bro?!" One of my teammates snapped at me, "Arroyo, you are so ghetto." What?! Me, ghetto? Not every Green Beret candidate grew up on the streets of Los Angeles, barely making it out of bondage. The majority are the best of the best, highly educated, and top performers. I'm sure if I tried thinking about it, I could fill pages of stories similar to this one. In full transparency, it took almost my entire 20-year career for me to change inside. It was lengthy because I hadn't fully submitted to God then. Like the Israelites, I had to remain in my wilderness until the old John died, and then I was free to cross over.

In the book of John, chapter 11, we read about Jesus resurrecting Lazarus from the dead. In verses 38-44 of that scene, God left us a treasure.

*38 Then Jesus, again groaning in Himself, came to the tomb. It was a cave, and a stone lay against it. 39 Jesus said, "**Take away the stone.**" Martha, the sister of him who was dead, said to Him, "Lord, by this time there is a stench, for he has been dead four days."*

40 Jesus said to her, "Did I not say to you that if you would believe you would see the glory of God?"

41 Then they took away the stone from the place where the dead man was lying. And Jesus lifted up His eyes and said, "Father, I thank You that You have heard Me.

42 And I know that You always hear Me, but because of the people who are standing by I said this, that they may believe that You sent Me."

*43 Now when He had said these things, He cried with a loud voice, "**Lazarus, come forth!**" 44 **And he who had died came out bound hand and foot with graveclothes, and his face was wrapped with a cloth. Jesus said to them, "Loose him, and let him go.**"*

The revelation I am sharing with you, a good friend shared with me. Then God exploded even more insight into my spirit. It's going to change your life. Think about what I have said up to this point. Leaving home for the military didn't change me internally. That took years and a lot of men and women speaking into my life and showing me a better way. Then, I had to surrender and let God heal me.

Back to the verses. Jesus is standing at the tomb of Lazarus and says, *"Take away the stone."* That is the very start of our freedom journey. Jesus has to remove the stone walls we set up around our hearts to protect us. Those walls keep others from getting in, including Jesus. He then calls Lazarus to come forth. What was dead is now alive. Like Lazarus, those who responded to Jesus have been resurrected in their spirit. Up to this point, the stone has been removed, and Lazarus has come forth. The scripture says Lazarus was bound hand and foot with graveclothes.

Stop! Think about the body of Christ, the people in the church. For billions of people, Jesus has removed the stone, and they've responded to His invitation for a relationship. Then why are so many still angry, mean, hurt, bitter, full of anxiety, depression, and fear? Because they are still bound hand and foot with graveclothes. It took Jesus telling those standing near, *"Loose him, and let him go."* The follow-on chapters will assist you in removing the graveclothes so you can live in freedom. Let me share one more insight before I hand over the conversation to Peggy Corvin.

We read in Luke 4:16-18 NLT:

"When he came to the village of Nazareth, his boyhood home, he went as usual to the synagogue on the Sabbath and stood up to read the Scriptures. [17] The scroll of Isaiah the prophet was handed to him. He unrolled the scroll and found the place where this was written:

"The Spirit of the LORD is upon Me,

*Because He has anointed Me (**Anointing**)*

*To preach the gospel to the poor; (**Salvation**)*

*He has sent Me to heal the brokenhearted, (**Healing**)*

*To proclaim liberty to the captives (**Freedom**)*

And recovery of sight to the blind, To set at liberty those who

*are oppressed; (**Transformation**)"*

Why didn't Jesus say, *"I am anointed to preach the gospel, and once people receive Me into their heart, then my mission is done."* Look at the verses in Luke 4:18. Preaching was only one part of His assignment. He had to remove the graveclothes by healing our broken hearts, setting captives free, returning our sight, and liberating the oppressed. Do you see what I am seeing? There are churches full of people bound in their graveclothes because it takes others to help loose them.

Several years ago, I asked some friends to pray for me because I had been battling stomach issues. While my friends were praying, someone said, "I don't believe it has to do with your stomach. Yes, that's the result, but I feel it's fear." They didn't know that I battled with anxiousness and fear for years. Jesus knew, and He was asking them to pull off those graveclothes. During the prayer, the symptoms immediately subsided. But they eventually returned. I began to pray, asking what was the root that was causing anxiety. God had me set up several freedom sessions with Peggy Corvin. During one of our sessions, God showed me where the fear originated. It happened when I was a young boy. After that session, the anxiety I battled for years never returned. When I met with Peggy, I was already serving in full-time ministry. What am I saying? We all live in this fallen world and have grave clothes, even ministers and celebrities you admire. You know who else has grave clothes on, your parents. Pray for them by asking God to send people they trust to loose them.

Peggy Corvin has a lot to share about her freedom journey. Then, she walks you through a comprehensive approach to get out of those graveclothes.

Like John, I had a powerful encounter with the Living God. Along the way, however, I have realized it began long before I was aware of His work in my life. His ministry is a process of unwrapping the things the world has wound around us to keep us from becoming what God created us to be. Looking back, every step of His process is clear and evident.

When I was thirteen, a friend invited me to go with her family to a small Missionary Baptist Church one Sunday night. That night after many verses of *Just As I Am*, I felt the warm Presence of God which compelled me to walk forward and pray with the Pastor. My friend and her mom were excited for me and told me everything would be so much better for me. I experienced His saving grace, but after the service, I went back home into the dysfunction caused by alcoholism and rage.

I had been adopted when I was five out of the deepest darkness and abuse a child can experience. My home life was now dominated by my wounded mother, who added another dimension to my soul wounds as her drunkenness regularly released unchecked rage. My awareness of His Presence faded, and I struggled through life without Him for two more decades. There were times when the fleeting memory of what I felt that Sunday night would come to mind, but I believed that even the God that my friend knew didn't want me *just as I was*; or any other way.

To Preach Good News To The Poor

By the time I was in my 30s, I made a plan to end my life and then set it in motion. I was no longer even sure He existed, but from deep inside me, a cry rose up to God. I had been on my knees but soon was lying face down, crying, and at the end of all desire for life. I wasn't asking for help, I just wanted Him to tell me how a mistake like me had ever been born. That is when I heard the good news of the gospel.

He came to me and told me He loved me and that He would always be with me. I experienced His Presence, His Light, and His Love. I have never been able to find words adequate enough to express what that time with Him was like. Natural words in any language fail to capture the Supernatural.

I was saved from the darkness of my life, and I knew it. Now I knew that when I did die, I would go to Heaven and finally live a happy life. Everything around me seemed different. There was more light in the world and more breath in the air around me, I felt like I could literally fly because I felt so light. I had no idea what to do next, so the following Sunday, I went to the church in town with the biggest steeple so they could show me.

I am grateful for my time in that church. I learned to "fellowship," and I learned how to serve. Fellowship meant having my Bible tucked into my left arm so I could extend the right hand of fellowship, keeping a smile on my face, and acting like everything was perfect in my life. Serving meant doing whatever needed to be done to keep the programs going. Often that looked like serving Kool-Aid at VBS, or ice cream at the Sunday night socials. However, the pastor of this church taught from the Bible and encouraged and compelled us to study it. It was His Word that began to cause me to want more.

In my understanding, being "Born Again" meant that all the old things from life were gone. I would never have to think about them again. Now, I was a new creation, and I lived in a Kingdom. In my mind, it should be like *Cinderella*. The prince came and took me away from the drudgery of meaningless life and the meanness inflicted by evil people. I was sure that He would change everything. All I had to do was show up at church to fellowship and serve and wait for Him to one day take me to Heaven. In the meantime, I was sure He would make my life happy; He would give me the desires of my heart. I had only one desire. I wanted a happy family, one in which I could love and be loved.

That seemed like a desire that would be readily provided by Him. Surely, I thought, He will give that to me; he will make my family happy and peaceful. I didn't doubt He wanted to change the dynamics of my family, but He went about it in an entirely different direction than I imagined.

Years after I encountered Him, hundreds of miles away from my core family, working in a new career and going to a new non-denominational church, I was terribly aggravated with Him. My family was a mess. There was always chaos, or drama, new hurts, or old situations dominating my thoughts and robbing me of my joy. My aggravation turned to anger, and I began to tell Him all about what I thought.

I was cleaning out old leftovers from my refrigerator as I had an internal rant directed at Him and explained why He should have made this different by now. After all, I read my Bible, never missed service, prayed all the time, and worked in church any time they needed me. In my opinion, I had done my part, so I wanted to know why had He not given me the desires of my heart!

As my mental rant continued, I pulled a carafe of old tomato juice out of the refrigerator. It was left over from a brunch I hosted, and I was irritated that all of it was left; not one drop was gone. I set it in the sink, turned the hot water on full force, and positioned the faucet over the top of it. I went back to wiping down refrigerator shelves, then returned to the sink.

The tomato juice still filled the carafe! I was stunned for a moment; this didn't make any sense. I turned off the water and stood in silence. Now that He had quieted me, He spoke, *"That is how you are with Me. You are so full of the old things from your past that there is no room for me to pour my Spirit into you."* I knew what He said was true. My nighttime dreams often called up past trauma. Raised voices made me want to cry and run away. Confrontation of any kind brought instant stomach aches. I held my breath and felt tense most days. I knew He was right, but I didn't want to face it.

He continued, *"I want to fill you with my Spirit, but you are clinging to the hurt and the heartbreak. Will you give them to me?"*

"I don't know if I can," was my honest whispered reply. *"I'm afraid if I go back and look at all that, I will start to cry; if I do, I don't think I will ever stop."*

That day, I stood in my kitchen where time seemed to stand still as I listened to the clock on the wall click off seconds. After a bit, I washed the carafe with water so hot it burned my hands, dried it, and set it on the shelf.

To Heal the Brokenhearted

He waited. He didn't force me. Weeks went by before I was finally confronted with the lies that I held as truth so strongly that I ran to Him and answered, *"Yes, I want to give all of this to you. I can't sort it out, make sense of it all, or move forward until You help me with it."* I was kneeling on the floor crying again, but this time, I reached for Life with everything in me. The Light of Life answered me. He began to gently open up the dark secrets I had in my broken heart, lift them out, and heal me.

This was a healing season for me. He took me back to the first time a lie had come into my soul. He showed me that He was there and answered all my hard questions about the situation. He then told me Truth that replaced each lie. As I worked with Him through all the brokenness of my life, I kept a "Master list" of the lies. Beside each one, I wrote the Scripture and the Rhema words He gave to me. I began to meditate on and memorize these, and over time, I came to believe them.

My major struggle was to be able to believe that I was loveable. The world had convinced me that I wasn't. He showered me with His presence and highlighted Scripture to show me how much He loved me. Whenever I would say something negative about myself, I would hear His voice ask, *"Whose child are you saying that about?"* Every day, I was amazed at His gentle, loving kindness, but He also kept me accountable. Oddly, it was His accountability that helped me know He loved me and wanted me to be in relationship with Him.

To Free the Oppressed

In the years to follow, He continued to heal my broken heart. With each healed hurt, He set me free from limiting myself and continued to show me the plan and purpose He had for me all along. Being free gave me the courage to love those around me. It was the ability to truly love that began to build my happy family. None of us are perfect, but we are imperfectly perfect for each other. This season of freedom was also a time when He sent so many of His other children into my life to mentor and encourage me.

To Open the Eyes of the Blind

I began to see everyone and everything in my life differently. With each level of freedom, I became less focused on myself and my world and began recognizing people around me struggling with heartbreak and soul wounds. When I stopped walking in my woundedness, I began to see others walking in theirs. It was amazing to me when he would use me to talk to strangers with compassion and speak Hope into their lives. Oftentimes, "church" happens at Walmart, gas stations, park benches, and in doctor's offices.

I began to pray daily that He would help me see the world the way He does. Walking with that awareness showed me more than I expected. While He walked on the earth, some of His strongest warnings were spoken to the highly religious. When we press in closer to Him, it seems we become sensitive to that same attitude.

He has placed me in four different, powerful churches led by strong, godly pastors and ministers. Each one produced spiritual growth and brought me skills and abilities I would never have had without them. They have been places of Heavenly encounters during corporate worship and Holy miracles as we seek Him together.

Because these places belong to Him and bring us closer and higher, they are often targeted by the enemy of the Kingdom and can be a source of hurtful wounding, too. I was trained to minister freedom in one of the largest church freedom programs. When we held two-day intense freedom encounters, the largest outpouring of pain from soul wounds came during our focus on father wounds. The second largest came from wounds from religion. So often, wounds caused by harsh words or painful rejection from someone in the church form lies and wrong beliefs about God's love. Particularly when someone is growing in their understanding of who they are, they can feel like God himself has rejected or shamed them.

Jesus said, *"God did not send His son into the world to condemn the world, but to save the world through Him."* Sometimes it seems that He has to save some of us from the churches. There is always grace to give, and even as we encourage others to walk close with God, we must do so centered on Jesus' new commandment to us all, *"Love one another, as I have loved you, you must love one another."* He loved us when there was nothing righteous about us; in fact, He still does. He has taught me that anytime I have gotten a "position" or opportunity to serve in a church, it is never "my" position. It's His church, and my job is to represent Him. Representing Him is being anointed.

The Spirit of The Lord Is Upon Me Because He Has Anointed Me To~
Free people following Him know how to finish that sentence for themselves. He has a unique place for us in His Kingdom. It is a place that completes our soul, brings us joy, and lets us soar with Him.

John and I work well together because we "see" His ministry process clearly. He highlighted it for each of us in His Word. We both have tremendous faith in His process to bring freedom to His children because our "faith" in it has become sight. We have seen countenances change, hearts soften, and thought patterns align with Truth as people are transformed. Both of us found great hope in the fact that Jesus went back to His boyhood home when He laid out His Ministry plan. He knew our hearts wanted transformation in our families, and He is the source of the change we see. We pray that the following chapters will help you find the courage to roll back the stone and get out of your grave clothes. He has far more attractive garments for us to wear.

Pause for a moment and listen. He is calling to **you**, saying, *"Come Forth!"* If you are ready to step into the life He has for you, press into these chapters designed to take the graveclothes off of you

זְדוֹרוֹ

Chapter Seven

Lo-debar's Lasting Effects

Are you still sitting in Lo-debar? Did you read The Truth chapter and feel your soul leap inside you? Yet, as you look at your life today, you are aware that your situation hasn't changed. If that is your experience, draw in close to these next chapters to seek new awareness about how your time in Lo-debar has cast a shadow over your life.

The Biblical Hebrew language contained approximately 7,000 words. Comparing that to the over 600,000 words available in the English language, you can easily see that each Hebrew word must have multiple uses and meanings. Hebrew names are significant and descriptive of people and places and can include many aspects of them.

When you examine the meanings of Lo-debar,[19] you find a fuller understanding that describes situations many of us experienced in our past. "Lo" means "no, none, or not." "Debar" can be translated as "pasture," which has deep meaning in the culture of David's time. If there is no pasture, then there is no shepherd. If there is no shepherd, there is no oversight or guidance. Without those, there is never a sense of safety or direction. Without those, the place is adrift in aimlessness

---

[19] BibleStudyTools.com

and chaos, so there is no purpose or provision—a lack of those results in meaningless hopelessness. With no shepherd, there is nothing to feed the sheep; thus, there is no life.

Debar, a transliteration of Debir, also means "word or communication." So, Lo-debar is a place where you never heard words your soul longed to hear. In a place of no communication, neither can you be heard. The chaos and confusion, the lies and the labels, the limitations swirling around you drowned out the Truth. That is why we find the recently redeemed Prince Mephibosheth identifying himself as a *"dead dog."*

That is also why so many Children of the Lord Most High, the Great, and Mighty King, stay bound to the past, even after they have met Him personally.

We come to faith through receiving a rhema word from God. He speaks a specific word to us in a way He knows we will understand, but with words that we have never heard spoken over us before. In his writing to the Romans, Paul said, *"So then faith comes by hearing, and hearing by the rhēma."*[20] The Greek word *rhēma*[21] means *"the Lord speaking His dynamic living word in a believer to in-birth their faith."* Many pastors, evangelists, parents, friends, neighbors, and ministers can tell us the word of God and create a desire in our hearts to know Jesus for ourselves. But they can't bring salvation to us. Only God can do that. When He speaks His specific living word to us, it changes us.

---

[20] God Calls us to Him, Romans 10:17, NKJV
[21] Strong's Concordance, Greek word #4487

If you just had this thought, *I have never heard my Heavenly Dad say anything to me;* then you have a longing in the deepest part of your soul for the sound of His word spoken over you. Ask Him with a true longing to hear from Him. He's your Dad. He will speak to you.

Holy Spirit will then create a desire to understand Jesus' *lógos* which means "reasoning expressed by written or spoken words, or a person speaking to share a message.".[22] This word is used 330 times in the New Testament as Jesus taught those around Him. Holy Spirit is the "breath of God." "*All Scripture is breathed out by God and profitable for teaching, for reproof, for correction, and for training in righteousness, that the man of God may be complete, equipped for every good work.*"[23]

It is through His Holy-Spirit-breathed words that God transforms our lives. He will still give rhema words to us because He loves us and wants us to always know He is right there. Sometimes, He will speak rhema words to us because there is an urgent need for us to hear him in that moment. He speaks to us through His *Logos* in Scriptures, so the teachings are always available to dig into and study so we know Him better.

He is speaking ~ Are you listening? Your Savior has come to you, opened the door to Kingdom life, and issued you an invitation to come feast with Him; yet you have found this Truth so amazing and so different from anything you have ever known, so very

[22] Strong's Concordance, Greek word, #3056
[23] The Living Word of God, The Bible, 2 Timothy 3:16-17, ESV

unbelievable, you are cringing in the shadows of your Lo-debar.

Many believers struggle for years to break free. However, you can't set yourself free. Your doctor can't set you free; neither can your Pastor, your friend, or anyone else. There are no seven steps to freedom, things to do, specific prayers to pray, or anything that will set you truly free. The words in this book cannot free you from the effects of your Lo-debar.

The words in this book have much better news for you. You can't break free because Jesus has already set you free. Jesus took EVERY sin that you have ever done and EVERY sin that has ever been *done to you*, He took the bitterness and the pain of those sins, and HE nailed them to the cross. Then He descended into hell and defeated the enemy of your soul. He took the keys to the gates of hell where curses made against you and your generations had been arranged. Now they are broken curses. He has fought hard and paid a huge price to give you freedom. He said, *"It is Finished!"*

The day you invited Him into your heart, the day you said, "Yes, Jesus, please come and be Lord of my life," on the day you submitted your soul to Him, you took your first step toward claiming the freedom He has won for you.

Our prayer is that you will get hungry enough for what He is offering you, that you will reach down inside your soul and find the courage to examine the lasting effects of your personal Lo-debar, bring them to the Light of Life, and be made whole.

It takes courage to go back and face the things that have hurt the deepest part of you. He understands that. He said, *"Have I not commanded you? Be strong and courageous, don't be afraid nor dismayed, for the Lord your God is with you wherever you go."*[24] This is a great statement of His faith in you. He will never command us to do things He knows we can't do. You *can* do this. Have the courage to be totally honest with yourself and Him, and feel those feelings you have always tried to push down inside. Be strong in your commitment to set aside time to be with Him, to study, memorize, and believe His Word. He will be with you every step, shining Truth into every shadow.

One important reason to reach down and find the courage is that when we give our lives to Him, He changes us and our households. When we surrender the strongholds by placing them on God's altar, He changes our future. Our changed life will breathe life into our family system and redeem God's promises over our coming generations.

The legacy of Saul and Jonathan was darkened by the events of the end of their lives. Mephibosheth carried their legacy forward. He was born into a royal legacy but lived in poverty, pain, and hopelessness in a dry and thirsty land. But then, he responded to the king, who called for him. At that point, he thought he was going to die. In a sense, he did. He died to the circumstances the world had created for him, but he was born again into a new and far better life. The king transformed the future of this wounded prince. He restored all the lands, gave him servants to work the land, and honored him

---

[24] Joshua 1:9, NKJV

with a place at the king's table for the rest of his life.

The name Mephibosheth is taken from two different Hebrew words. The first is "pa'ah" which means to cleave into pieces, and the second is "bosheth" which means shame. His name means "dispeller of shame." Dispel means to cause to vanish. So, Mephibosheth is a "shame destroyer" or "image breaker."

How very like Our Father to make sure we came to know this story. We are encouraged by it because our journey has been similar. This tells us that the shame and the tarnished image we have struggled with can vanish when we surrender to Our King. Our future will be radically different. Since He is a generational God, He promised to fulfill his everlasting covenant for us and for those in our generations coming after us.

Read the account in the book of Acts of a man who found out He is still intentional about our generations. There, we find a jailer who thought he would surely die when God freed Paul and Silas. But the goodness of God kept the other prisoners from leaving. In humble gratitude, the jailer falls to the ground and cries out, *"Sirs, what must I do to be saved?* He had not asked about his family. But God has Paul tell him, *"Believe on the Lord Jesus Christ, and you will be saved, you and your household."* [25] If you want to see your family saved and transformed, draw in and let God get the "Lo-debar" out of you. Holy Spirit will also redeem and transform our generations through our redemption and transformation.

---

[25] Paul and Silas in the Jail at Midnight, Acts 16: 25-34, NKJV

In the following chapters, the most common effects of Lo-debar will be identified and examined so they can be <u>defeated</u>. Through this, you can satisfy the hunger for His Truth and your desire to stop living in the shadows instead of His Kingdom. You can then stand fully in His Presence and *know* who you are.

The journey begins by asking Him to be with you and being willing to talk to and listen to what He will say to you about your Lo-debar.

דְרוֹר

Chapter Eight

Courtroom of Your Heart

Imagine being Mephibosheth as he hears someone has been sent to pick him up and bring him to the king.

He was five years old when a nurse picked him up amid chaos, and in a rush to escape death, she dropped him. In one sudden moment, he was stripped of everything that defined him. His grandfather, who was also his king, was gone; his father was gone, his home and the kingdom around him were gone. His physical ability was forever limited. His very identity was stripped away. He was no longer a prince with privilege; he was crippled and confined to live in a ghetto. He was a young, innocent child with no voice or vote in the actions of others, which had set this trajectory of his life into play. What do you think was in his heart?

Was he mad at all Philistines for killing his father and grandfather to the point that he hated them all? Did he blame his dad for leaving that day and going to fight them instead of taking care of him? Was he bitter at the clumsy nurse who tripped and dropped him? As Mephibosheth sat all these years, watching his muscles atrophy, did he loathe himself? Did he have intense fear, dread, and distrust whenever anyone came to carry him someplace? Had he lived every day of his life just waiting to be killed by this new king since that was the way of the world? When he thought of kings, did he imagine vengeful, punishing warmongers greedily taking from others and never giving?

What do you suppose were the longings of Mephibosheth's heart?

Had King Saul ever affirmed him as a prince? Did he try to follow Jonathan around so he could be just like him? Did he hope every day that his dad might tell him he did a good job? Did people around him listen to his dreams and help make them even bigger? Did the nurse ever tell him how sorry she was for dropping him? Were there any people who told him he *could still do* many things even though he could no longer walk? Had anyone ever told him how much he was loved?

How had his Lo-debar experience shaped the person he had become?

We don't have the privilege of knowing what was inside this crippled prince. We do, however, know what was inside the king who was sending for him. The king who called him to his table so he could restore and redeem his inheritance was acting out of love for Jonathan and honor for Saul, the man who had served God as king. David was a man after God's own heart.

Today, God's heart is calling you to come deeper and be close to Him.

The thoughts and feelings that Mephibosheth may have held in his heart are also very real effects that can be in our lives. All of the things his soul wanted to hear are desires of all of our hearts.

Our heart is the very center of our inner person. Our heart is the place where we store memories, thoughts, reflections, and resolutions based on our experiences. It is where our soul (the mind, emotions, and will) stores essential parts of our lives that shape and direct who we are. It is where we form our beliefs.

Beliefs are the content of our hearts and have dominion over our thoughts. Thoughts reside in our brains and have words attached to them. You can put language to them. Beliefs often have no language attached, but they are firmly rooted in our hearts. Before we have a saving encounter with Jesus, we have a belief system in our hearts that has been created by the world where we live. When things happen, we form a thought about our world based on that situation. In the midst of traumatic events, we come to believe a lie. We then develop an ungodly belief based on the lie. That belief will shadow our future interactions with people.

An ungodly belief will appear to be true based on the facts of a person's experience, yet it is absolutely false based on God's Word. It is not uncommon for a person to be oblivious to lies they believe because they seem to be true based on the world around them.

Mephibosheth's father left for war, leaving the boy in the care of a nurse. When his father never returned, he could have drawn a conclusion about his father. The lie may have been that if his father had loved him, he would not have left him. From that lie, he could have then formed the belief that seemed evident to him. He could have believed that fathers who love their children always protect and take care of them. He then could form the belief that since his dad didn't protect him, then he was obviously an unlovable son.

When the nurse dropped him, it would have been proof to his mind that he was unlovable. After all, if she had loved him, she would have taken better care of him. Children have no way of knowing what is going on in the lives of the adults taking care of them, so their judgments are based only on the world as they know it.

If we don't know Jesus intimately, our identity is based on our worldly belief system. C. S. Lewis states it perfectly, *"The more we get what we now call "ourselves" out of the way and let Him take us over, the more truly ourselves we become. The more I resist Him and try to live on my own, the more I become dominated by my own heredity and upbringing and surroundings and natural desires."*[26] When all we know is what is going on in and through the people and situations in our lives, the less we know about who we are.

When we meet Jesus, we are filled with Spiritual life. When that happens, Spirit and soul reside in our hearts. There is often a transitional time when our soul is still dominated by the ungodly belief system deeply rooted in us. None of that agrees with Holy Spirit. Godly belief systems agree with the word of God, reveal His very nature and character to us, and guide us to live the life He planned for us. Our soul has entrenched thoughts, feelings, and a set of responses based on past experiences that dominate our behavior.

The Apostle Paul sums up this state of transformation very well, *"I have discovered this principle of life - that when I want to do what is right, I inevitably do what is wrong. I love God's law with all*

---

[26] C. S. Lewis, *Mere Christianity*, California, Harper CA, 2001

my heart. But there is another power within me that is at war with my mind. This power makes me a slave to the sin that is still within me. Oh, what a miserable person I am! Who will free me from this life that is dominated by sin and death? Thank God! The answer is in Jesus Christ our Lord. So, you see how it is: In my mind, I really want to obey God's law, but because of my sinful nature I am a slave to sin."[27]

We have a place of deciding our responses to events in life called "**the courtroom of our heart**." We look at the evidence, we weigh our experiences, we remember what happened the last time we encountered this thing, and we decide what judgment we will make. We then act on our decision, and that shapes our character and answers our inner question, "Who am I, really?"

This and the next three chapters address the most common effects of our Lo-debar experiences. These first ones, unforgiveness and bitterness, are two of the most vile, chaos-causing, pain-inflicting, life-stifling shadows cast into our souls.

Writing this, I imagine many of you groaning, "Not this again!" If that is you, remember Jesus is with you, He has set you free, and you are reading this so you can live in the wholeness and freedom He is offering.

Forgiveness is an often-taught topic from the pulpit. It is something many of us have said we will do yet failed in our trying. Even when we are parroting Jesus' words, *"Father, forgive them for they don't know what they are doing."[28]* Deep in our souls, we may

---

[27] The Apostle Paul, Romans 7:21-25, NLT
[28] Jesus while being nailed to the cross, Luke 23:34, NLT

harbor hidden thoughts. *Yes, they did know what they were doing! I did not deserve what happened to me. I was the one left to walk in despair. I lived covered in shame, which they should wear.* These and other obviously "un-Christian" thoughts run through our souls. We think these things, respond with feelings about them, and fortify our wills to act accordingly.

Every time we hear a sermon teaching that forgiveness is a decision we **MUST** make because Jesus chose to forgive us, we usually tighten our resolve. We white-knuckle it and often repeat, "I **will** forgive them, I **will** forgive them," until it takes on the cadence and pace of "the little train that could" phrase. "I think I can; I think I can."

That will sometimes shush the cry for justice that keeps springing up in our heart, *at least for a while."*

Part of our struggle with forgiveness is caused by the fact that we don't fully understand Jesus' teachings on this subject. Anytime we are studying Scripture, we must understand the context.

When we are "New Testament" Christians, we risk missing God's true nature and character, which is, in part, revealed to us in the Old Testament too. He has never changed. He never will. He is the God of Creation, He is the God of the flood, He is the one who parted the waters, He walked on the water, He went to the wilderness with His children, and He went to the gates of hell and took the keys. He prompted the writings found in the Old and the New Testaments. He is the same God who created you in your mother's womb, the One who is standing with you today, and will be the same God who holds you in His arms the moment you take your last breath here on earth.

To look to the root of unforgiveness, we must consider that Jesus came to earth at the exact time Father God wanted Him to, to the people He wanted Him to teach, to achieve the eternal purpose designed for Him. He was born into the generational line of King David. He was Jewish and came to bring the message of salvation to the Jewish people. He memorized the Scrolls. He taught from those by the time He was twelve. He spoke Torah Truth to defeat satan in the wilderness at the beginning of His earthly ministry. He was harsh to those who had taken the teachings and turned them into manmade rules. He came to show everyone that the laws He came to fulfill were valid and were written to bring us into a relationship with God and other people. [29] It is through those laws that we can fulfill the greatest commandment. [30]

Forgiveness started the day God cast Adam and Eve out of Eden. It was finished the day Jesus rose from the tomb. He showed us every step of the way what He means by forgiveness because he knew we would live in a broken, hurting world until He came again to establish His Kingdom on Earth.

We know the story of Adam and Eve. Eve yielded to the temptation to try to take the place of God and invited Adam to join her. By partaking in the fruit of the Tree of Knowledge of Good and Evil, they revealed they wanted to rule their world based on what they thought was the good thing to do. We only have to take a brief look

---

[29] Jesus' teaching about the Law, Matthew 5:17-20, NLT
[30] Jesus' Greatest Commandment teaching, Matthew 22:37-40, NLT

around us today to see that same attitude prevalent in our world and notice the mess it has made in our lives.

God sent them out of the garden so they wouldn't live forever in their fallen state of delusion about their own goodness. They must once again come to know their great need for Him to rule in their life. Just before He sent them out, He took off the fig leaves, which they had decided were good things to wear, and He clothed them in animal skins.

Don't miss the importance of that act. As we consider it, the significance of that single act becomes clear. God had given Adam the task of naming all the animals. Naming is a significant job that is important to God. As Adam learned and understood each animal, he would give them an appropriate name. Standing at the point of eviction from paradise, Adam and Eve would have clearly and deeply understood the cost of their sin.

The skins God gave them that day were taken from the same animals they had tended and gotten to know. They felt the wages of their sin as they put on the skins. God was illustrating the death that sin always brings. Hopes, dreams, relationships, opportunities, and life itself die when sin is allowed to rule in our lives. He *requires* the sinner to make an act of sacrifice to acknowledge the gravity of their actions. He carried out the first sacrifice, and He carried out the last.

The Bible records stories of mankind and their continued journey away from God; then, with their confession, repentance, and sacrifice, they return to Him. Throughout the Old Testament, the ancient men acknowledged that **all** sin is against God. His ways are the ones we are breaking. With the coming of our Savior, animal sacrifices are no longer required. However, when we focus only on mercy and grace, we tend to overlook the teachings about confession and repentance. We lose sight, miss the pain, and don't consider the excruciating cost of the sacrifice He made for us.

He was rejected, reviled, beaten to the brink of death, then hung on a cross in naked shame and jeered while slowly dying a horrifically painful death. What had he done? He had chosen to do the only thing He could do to step into eternity and lift the wages of my sin off me and yours off you so we can be forgiven. He wants us in Heaven with Him. He also wants us to walk in His Presence and experience His Kingdom while we are on Earth.

Jesus said, *"If you are bringing your sacrifice and remember that your brother has something against you, leave your sacrifice there, go and be reconciled to your brother, then come and offer your gift."*[31]

Each morning, as we offer our life to Jesus as our living sacrifice, He wants us to consider the state of the life He has given us. How have we handled the precious things from Heaven He has placed in our life? What He treasures most are people, and when He places someone in our life, He entrusts the care of that person to us. When we thoughtlessly, carelessly hurt someone, Holy Spirit prompts sorrow in our hearts. Sincere Godly sorrow causes tender pain in our hearts. We hurt when we have hurt someone. Here in His teaching,

---

[31] Jesus in His Sermon on the Mount, Matthew 5:23-24, NLT

Jesus commands us with a sense of urgency to go to the person, confess that we know we did wrong, offer acts of repentance, and ask for their forgiveness so we can be reconciled to them; then, we can be reconciled to Him.

Sinners were and still are called to repent, confess to those they have harmed, and make restitution when they should and can. There is mercy and grace offered to those who do this. Admitting our sins and asking for forgiveness from those we have harmed is an important step that builds relationships and allows us back into close communion with God. It is the way we can walk with Him in His kingdom now. We honor Him when we honor those He put in our lives.

This is one of those places where we must hold on to the courage He commanded us to have and lean on Him as we learn to openly confess to someone we have hurt. We all hurt people sometimes. When we follow His teachings, we strengthen our character and grow relationships.

He further instructed us to go to someone who has hurt us and tell them how we feel. He gives great detail in Matthew 18 about going alone, and if the person who hurt us doesn't listen, then we must go back and take some witnesses. This teaching can be challenging for anyone with a deeply entrenched desire to avoid all conflict. The Scripture is clear; the goal is to confront the person with their need to repent and to be willing to offer God's forgiving love when they do.

By understanding that these critical teachings are given to us to help us have healthy relationships, we can grow in our ability to find our voice and speak up when people hurt us. Usually, in the very act of communication, a new and higher understanding will be gained for everyone, and the relationship will be strengthened. We get to know people more intimately when we can be honest and forthright and seek to understand. God's ways consistently surpass the results we expect.

In the teaching that we must forgive to be forgiven, Jesus instructs Christians.[32] We must be ready to offer forgiveness to those who have sinned against us when they come in repentance and humbly ask. When we accept Jesus as our Savior, that is how God forgives us; we come, confess, and repent. It is what He does when we confess our failings daily, change how we live, and seek Him. He expects us to do the same for others.

But what do you do when no one from your dark past has ever come asking you to forgive them? That is the key to forgiveness. Jesus paid the price for all sin, but His forgiveness is given to those who come, confess, repent, and then gratefully receive it. When that hasn't happened, does that mean we don't have to forgive them? He definitely is not telling us to hold on to the unforgiveness and the bitterness it brought into our hearts. He wants us to draw near to Him so He can help us get past all of it.

What we honestly want is justice. We want to matter. We want them to care about us enough to admit that what they did was wrong. Or acknowledge that what they should have done but didn't do hurt

---

[32] Jesus, Teaching about the Lord's Prayer, Matthew 6:9-15, NLT

the deepest part of us. We want them to suffer because they made us suffer. We want to hold court in our hearts and find them guilty.

We can testify endlessly about the depth of the abuse, the betrayal, public shame and humiliation, the physical pain, the ridicule, and the demeaning way we were treated. We can testify about the deep sad silence in our souls that echoes the unmet need for love and acceptance.

We can also judge them. They were horribly wrong to mistreat an innocent child. Going through our list, we can find every single one of them guilty. We can also sentence them. They had no right to live their life as if we had never mattered, to never acknowledge the pain they had caused. The cry of our hearts is that they must be held accountable.

When we get honest about what is in our hearts, Jesus is right there. He knows about it all. He understands! He has cried with us; He aches with us today. Yet, He asks us to transfer all of that out of our hearts by giving it to Him. *"Vengeance is Mine,"* He says. We can find peace in that. If we have stored bitterness in our hearts, we may add, *All right! You go, God! You get 'em! Give them what they deserve! Smite 'em!*

However, consider what Paul wrote to Timothy. *"There is one God and one Mediator who can reconcile God and humanity—the man Christ Jesus. He gave his life to purchase freedom for everyone."*[33]

---

[33] Apostle Paul to Timothy about the why behind Jesus' sacrifice, 1 Timothy 2:5, NLT

Jonah wouldn't go to Nineveh because he knew they would turn to Him and be redeemed if he told them about God. He judged them in the courtroom of his heart and decided they didn't deserve God's redemption.

When people have hurt us deeply, we can understand how Jonah felt. God, who loves us with an everlasting love, doesn't want even one single person to be lost. Some of the people who were entrusted with our care are people who have wounded people their whole life. Often what is stored in our hearts is bitterness against them, and we can become so hardened that we honestly believe they don't deserve forgiveness. When we believe that, *we are right*. They don't deserve it. But then, none of us deserve it. We can never earn the salvation, grace, mercy, and love that is ours as a free gift because of Jesus' sacrifice.

It is deeply wounded people who wound others. When we honestly examine our life, we usually discover that we have hurt others out of our woundedness. We hurt other people because of the hurt done to us. Perhaps all those from the darkness who hurt you did what they did because of what people had done to them. Could that be what was behind their action?

What will happen if you take them out of the courtroom in your heart and give them over to God's courtroom? He is the only *just* Judge. Can you release them to God, knowing He would save them if it is at all possible?

The realization is that if He saves them, they will be changed. None of us can meet Him and not be changed. With Him in their heart, they would feel sorry for what they had done. They would know you mattered. There would be justice.

God is not a weak god who allows sin to slide. He will chase everyone right up to the gates of hell itself, offering salvation to transform darkened souls into the child of God they are intended to be. He will also turn them over to their rebellious ways if they insist on being hell-bound.

But only He can make the judgment call.

There is another, called the accuser, who pronounces lies over all of God's creations to stop them from becoming who God meant for them to be. He is the father of the lies that echo in our hearts, the perpetrator of pain, the enemy of our soul, and the source of all dark things that shadow our lives. He is the one who wants us to continue focusing our thoughts, feelings, and will on wanting to condemn others. When all our emotional energy, thoughts, and self-will are focused on that, we will never become the powerful, amazing, influential person our Creator made us to be.

As we sit on the bench as judges in the courtroom of our hearts, we must decide who we will agree with over these people who have hurt us. If we stand and continue to accuse, we give up all our power to become who we are meant to be. We will choose to wear the label "Victim!" calling out, "See, see how crippled I am! They did that to me; this is their fault!" Instead of claiming our "Victor's Crown" available to us from the one who paid the price for all sin, the one calling out, *Come follow Me.* The one who loves us with an everlasting love and who needs every one of us to participate in building His

Kingdom. He is the one who has earned the right to the Glory for our lives. Why would we choose to make the dark one famous instead of Him?

When we agree to release them into the care of God, we will be making room in our hearts for His Spirit so we can be healed from the wounds they left. He came to bind up our broken hearts. He wants to help us remove the shattered pieces so they will stop inflicting more pain. He wants us to stop drinking the bitter poison killing our true life.

He wants to take the darkest parts out of our hearts. As He does, we will find He respects and honors us; He never minimizes any of it. He hurts when we hurt; as we process this with Him, He lets us know He hasn't forgotten about any of it. He also lets us know He genuinely cares. He is a just and holy God who reassures us, instills us with security, and restores our hope.

Released from the heavy burden of judging and punishing others, we begin to see people differently. It is sometimes difficult to see the truth of who people are in Christ because it is hard to see beyond what they are doing. No redemption is offered as long as we either condemn them by labeling them *as their sin* or believe that what they are doing is the limiting fact of *who they truly are.*

Are you a wounded child of a wounded child? If so, your life may be diminished by your wounds and the belief system in your soul. Do you have unforgiveness and bitterness in your heart that is a heavy shadow over your life? As you consider that question, also remember you can't set yourself free from it. No other person can either. Only

Jesus can help you with this. But the great news is that He is always with you and willing to work on this when you invite Him into this situation. Also, He wants your freedom even more than you do! He died to prove it!

The chains of unforgiveness are most commonly tied to abusive, neglectful, or distant parents. This may also include authority figures who failed as protectors or providers, such as pastors, coaches, or other guardians. Siblings, close peers from childhood, or trusted friends are the next most common group of people causing bitterness in our hearts. Those who hurt us so deeply that they added an extra layer of pain because of their betrayal can make forgiveness doubly difficult.

The last section of the book has a guided exercise to help you release any people who never acknowledged to you that they had hurt you. If you have ongoing pain and repeating patterns, we want to encourage you to pause your progress in this book, find that section, and let God come work with you so you can be set free.

Sometimes, the hardest person to forgive is ourselves. In this instance, there is added far-reaching pain because a person often deals with regret. *If only I hadn't. . .* or *If only I had. . .* This is also very hard because we know we don't deserve forgiveness. But it is important to remember that no one does.

"But now God has shown us a way to be made right with him without keeping the requirements of the law, as was promised in the writings of Moses and the prophets long ago. We are made right with God by placing our faith in Jesus Christ. And this is true for everyone

who believes, no matter who we are. For everyone has sinned; we all fall short of God's glorious standard. Yet God, in his grace, freely makes us right in his sight. He did this through Christ Jesus when he freed us from the penalty for our sins."[34]

Perhaps the most difficult to admit, however, is unforgiveness directed at God. Many believe He caused the trouble because He was mad at us. Sometimes, we believe He could have prevented the problem, but He chose not to do that for us. This journey to wholeness begins with finding the courage to draw near to God and ask Him to talk to you about those thoughts and feelings.

It is critical to pour this out in honest talks with Him. His love for you is far greater than you can even imagine. He is the one who created you. He will talk with you about your situation. We pray that you will have the courage to talk with Him and listen to what you hear. There is often anger toward Him in these situations; the next chapter will go into greater depth about this. We also can ask Him to send someone into our life to be a spiritual minister to guide us in these hard places. It is hard to talk to the one you find hard to forgive.

So, as was stated above, if we can't do this, how can we possibly get past this bitterness? We do it prayerfully, trusting in the One who can.

Begin by asking Him to help you *want* to break this bondage of unforgiveness out of your heart. Tell Him you can't do this without Him. Be transparent with Him; He knows it all, but He wants us to

---

[34] The Apostle Paul, Romans 3:21-24, NLT

trust Him enough to share everything with Him. Tell Him how it hurt. Tell Him how sad you are inside your heart because this happened. Tell Him all the ways it has kept you from being fully alive and participating in the life He has for you. Tell Him why you haven't been able to forgive. Tell Him everything. Don't hold back your feelings; they are important to Him. He has feelings, too. He gets sad and cries when hard things happen.[35]

Once you have poured it all out, ask Him the hard questions. *Jesus, do you care what happened to me? Where were you? What do you think of the situation? Will you give me revelations about this and show me the truth?*

Don't rush this time with Him. You may have many more questions as you seek the Lord in this situation. One question that is always very important in all our situations is, *"Lord, how can I participate with You to bring about the results You have for me?"* Pay close attention to the answer you hear. It may seem unusual, and you may resist it at first. *His ways are not our ways,* so we must grab the courage and be willing to follow what He tells us.

What has your soul longed to hear? The desire of His heart is for you to hear those words. Talk to the one who is bending down from Heaven waiting for you so He can be with you.[36]

Work with Him in every area where you are holding unforgiveness. Give them over to Him; He can be trusted with the outcome. Once you have reached the place of forgiveness, speak it

---

[35] The Account of Jesus Raising Lazarus, John 11, NLT
[36] A Psalm of David, Psalm 53:2, NLT

aloud. Tell Jesus, "I forgive. . ." Complete it with who you forgive and for what. Remember, it is only through His power that you can do this. Be sure to thank Him for the work He has done with you in this.

If you are holding unforgiveness against yourself, approach it the same way. You will have to personalize it and guard against discounting the forgiveness Jesus has for you since you might think you don't deserve it. Remember Saul, who later became Apostle Paul? He was condemning God's children with a passionate vengeance. Jesus came to him and said, *"Saul! Saul! Why are you persecuting me?"*[37] He might well ask you that same question if you continue to condemn yourself. After all, you are one of His precious children. Talk to Him about this.

In your heart is also where your will lives. Holy Spirit will never force you to do anything, but He will always empower you to get free. You will always have a choice.

Consciously decide to give it all to Holy Spirit and release the pain and the power of the offense from your heart. Activate your will to guard your heart so that the enemy of your soul can't put any of the old thoughts or memories into your heart! It's YOUR heart, and the enemy has no claim on it. Stand your ground in your new-found freedom.

Be sure to see if there is any residual Root of Bitterness. Forgiveness work is never complete if we leave bitterness in our souls.

---

[37] The Conversion of the Apostle Paul, Acts 9, NLT

Consider the walk to the cross and remember what Jesus endured before he even became our sin. He was betrayed by Judas, by His Disciples, by the Jews, and by the crowds.

He was scourged, which means he was beaten severely with twelve or thirteen whips tied together with stones and glass in them.

"When Pilate had scourged Jesus, he delivered Him to be crucified. Then the governor's soldiers took Jesus and gathered the whole company of soldiers around him. They stripped him and put a scarlet robe on him, and then twisted together a crown of thorns and set it on his head. They put a staff in his right hand. Then they knelt in front of him and mocked him. "Hail, king of the Jews!" they said. They spit on him, and took the staff and struck him on the head again and again. They led him to Golgotha where they offered Jesus wine to drink, mixed with gall, but after tasting it, he refused to drink it."[38]

Remember, Jesus is God, but at this point, he is walking as a man because of His great love for us - He is choosing to take all of this punishment for us. Also, at this point, all of our sin has not been laid on Him.

He tasted bitterness at this point in the journey, but **he refused to drink it.** He would have been bitter toward us if he had taken it in as a man.

Jesus refused to take it in. It reminds us that we will taste bitterness in this journey – but we don't have to drink it in; we can refuse to let it poison our souls.

---

[38] The Account of the Crucifixion of Jesus, John 19, NLT

In the book of Matthew, we find, *"Now from the sixth hour until the ninth hour there was darkness over all the land. And about the ninth hour Jesus cried out with a loud voice, saying, "Eli, Eli, lama sabachthani?" that is, "My God, My God, why have You forsaken Me?"* ~~Up until now, He had called Him ABBA.

He became sin; my sin, your sin, every sin ever committed by and against us. For three hours, it was all laid on Him until He became all sin.

God is HOLY. The sin laid on Jesus separated Jesus from God. Now look at what John records.

"After this, knowing that <u>all</u> <u>things</u> were now accomplished, that the Scripture might be fulfilled, Jesus said, **"I thirst!"** *Now a vessel full of bitter wine was sitting there; and they filled a sponge with bitter wine, put it on hyssop, and put it to His mouth. So, <u>when Jesus had received the gall</u>, He said, "It is finished!" And bowing His head, He gave up His spirit."*[39]

How powerful to see that He was very intentional about taking the bitterness that was a residual part of the sin that so dramatically impacts all our lives. He knew he was only one second away from death; He would not have needed anything to drink. This is to make an everlasting point for all of us who have dealt with deep pain and its bitterness.

I believe that today Jesus is saying something your soul has longed to hear.

---

[39] John 19:30, NKJV

"I love you, and you are precious to me. I took your sin, and I took the bitterness of the results of that sin. I took the sin done against you – terrible things that were hurtful and wrong, but I paid the price for that so that You can let it go. And I took the bitterness about that sin. I took it, Precious One, because I don't want that to be what your life is about. I want to give you the fullness of My Joy, so I took the power that the consequences of sin have in your life. I don't want you to walk under the shadow of that any longer. You can leave it here at the cross where it has been paid for, and you can take up my promises and walk in newness with Me. It is finished; I have set you Free!"

The case has been decided in His courtroom. What about in yours? Our prayer for you is that today is the day that you will bang your gavel and proclaim, "Case dismissed!"

זְווּר

Chapter Nine

The Deep Shadow of Anger

We know that we are created in the image of God. As we spend time in Scripture, there is no mistaking the fact that Father God exhibits His anger. There are many Scriptures about His Wrath, which brings about punishment and destruction. As beings created in His image, we can have anger as a reaction to situations in our lives. Our problem with anger is that we are not holy like God is, and we misuse our anger.

We may as well address this first because it is the go-to example people use when someone confronts them on their wrong use of anger. *But Jesus, who was perfect, got angry when He cleansed the temple!* Yes, He did. Looking at His earthly life and ministry, we can see many times when He grew frustrated with His disciples and rebuked them on occasion. His wrath was made apparent to the religious leaders of His day; they just didn't understand that it wasn't all about their man-made rules. It is, and has always been, about our relationship with God.

In fact, His greatest, most often cited expression of righteous anger was because of what they were allowing to happen at the Temple. That's when He showed just how angry He was. There are actually two different times that He came in and "cleaned house" in the Temple. Both have some important insights into anger when we study them within the context of those verses.

The first happened in the early days of His ministry.[40] Shortly after he performed his first miracle at the wedding in Cana, he rested for a few days with his family, then went to Jerusalem for the Passover. When He got to the Temple, He found all the dishonest trading in a significant area.

The Temple was sacred to the Jews and was highly regulated. People who were not Jewish were banned from the Temple, with only one exception. They were allowed to enter the Court of the Gentiles but were forbidden to go any farther than that outer court. The inner Temple courtyards were closed off and had notices at the entrances, warning foreigners and uncircumcised persons that crossing into one of the other courtyards was punishable by death.

The whole reason God had "a chosen people group" was so He could teach them how to live so that He could bless them abundantly. He knew the other people around them would notice the difference in the Israelites' lives and be drawn to Him, too. He made Israel to be a nation of priests, prophets, and missionaries so they could teach others about Him.

That is the desire of His heart. He wants to be our God, and He wants us to be His children. He wants us to live abundantly blessed with all the good things of life. He also wants us to tell others about what it is like having Him in our life and to invite all other people into the kingdom.

---

[40] Jesus Clears the Temple, John 2:13-22, NLT

When Jesus got to the Temple, he found that instead of opening the Court of the Gentiles for worship and prayer for anyone not Jewish, the leaders used it to make a big profit from this heavy turnout for Passover. But Jesus did not have a knee-jerk reaction and fly off the handle. Look how John recorded the action.

"Jesus found in the Temple those who sold oxen and sheep and doves, and the money changers doing business. <u>When</u> <u>He</u> <u>had</u> <u>made</u> <u>a</u> <u>whip</u> <u>of</u> <u>cords</u>, He drove them all out of the temple, with the sheep and the oxen, and poured out the changers' money and overturned the tables. He said to those who sold doves, "Take these things away! Do not make My Father's house a house of merchandise!" [41]

Throughout His ministry, Jesus only did what His Father told Him to do; He only said what His Father told Him to say. We see He took time to find the materials and make a whip to emphasize His point. He was in constant communication with the Father. We see in this illustration that when His anger arose, He probably got instructions on how to handle the situation, then went and made the whip to properly emphasize his lesson. His mission on earth was to carry out Our Father's mission decided in Heaven, and God had said His house would be *a house of prayer for all nations.*[42]

Was Jesus angry? Absolutely. Did He **re**act in rage? No, He **acted** to make sure His point was made, and He did it appropriately. He used it as a teachable moment, the way the Father wanted.

---

[41] Jesus cleanses the Temple. John 2:13-16, NLT; further references Matt. 21:12-13; Mark 11:15-17; Luke 19:45-48, NLT
[42] Our Father describes His Temple, Isaiah 56:7, NLT

Anger is not wrong. It is the misuse of anger that often harms other people, and that is always wrong.

Anger is very often a mask emotion used to cover over the real pain. Anger is often referred to as an iceberg because the outpouring of anger is the tip; it is the visible thing we see. However, it is frequently directed at something other than the real source of the problem. The angry behavior that is readily seen is usually triggered by many things that are beneath the surface. The soul wounds left unhealed are much broader and deeper than the anger.

If you are dealing with rage, sudden outbursts of anger, or always have anger just below the surface of your soul, you may have a shadow from your Lo-debar that looks like anger, but it may be rooted in fear, abandonment, and reactions to the trauma you have been through.

When a situation triggers anger, our bodies have a physical reaction. We tense up and are very hyper-alert to everything, and anger can feel more significant than it really is once we calm down. When trauma happens, one of the residual effects can be that we live in a tense state. Sometimes, we may find that we are holding our breath, our shoulders are tight for no apparent reason, or our stomach feels tied in knots. The shadow from the past may be from living in the chaos of Lo-debar, where there was no shepherd, so you believe that you must always be alert to protect yourself and stay in control of your circumstances.

If you came through chaos because there were no established rules and no one made you feel safe, you might get unduly angry when others break the rules. When we do this, other people respond angrily and set up the cycle again. This reinforces lies that have informed our decisions and then keeps us locked in behavior that uses anger to make people "behave" so we can feel safe.

Sometimes, deep hurt comes from people we should have been able to trust to protect and provide for us. The anger that comes from that is often a defense mechanism. Anger is definitely a tool that pushes people away so they can't hurt us. The lie-believed-as-truth keeps whispering to your soul that you can't let people get close to you because they will hurt you if you do. The problem is we have been created to live in relationships with others. We can't find peace in our hearts until we let Jesus in to heal these hurt places so we can live the life He wants for us.

Scripture is full of examples of anger between siblings. If these relationships and the wounds from the past aren't healed, they can be a constant source of reactive anger. The source of the hurt ranges from negative, hurtful words to physical abuse or neglect.

During his childhood, David dealt with pain inflicted by his family's attitudes toward him and directly from words from a brother. Many of us can relate to his story as told in *The Message*.[43]

"God addressed Samuel: "So, how long are you going to mope over Saul? You know I've rejected him as king over Israel. Fill your flask with anointing oil and get going. I'm sending you to Jesse of Bethlehem. I've spotted the very king I want among his sons."

---

[43] David's Anointing, and Battle with Goliath, 1 Samuel 16–17, MSG

"I can't do that," said Samuel. "Saul will hear about it and kill me."

God said, "Take a heifer with you and announce, 'I've come to lead you in worship of God, with this heifer as a sacrifice.' Make sure Jesse gets invited. I'll let you know what to do next. I'll point out the one you are to anoint."

Samuel did what God told him. When he arrived at Bethlehem, the town fathers greeted him apprehensively. "Is there something wrong?"

"Nothing's wrong. I've come to sacrifice this heifer and lead you in the worship of God. Prepare yourselves, be consecrated, and join me in worship." He made sure Jesse and his sons were also consecrated and called to worship.

When they arrived, Samuel took one look at Eliab and thought, "Here he is! God's anointed!"

But God told Samuel, "Looks aren't everything. Don't be impressed with his looks and stature. I've already eliminated him. God judges persons differently than humans do. Men and women look at the face; God looks into the heart."

Jesse then called up Abinadab and presented him to Samuel. Samuel said, "This man isn't God's choice either."

Jesse kept presenting sons, and Samuel kept declining them as king material. Can you imagine each one? Was there a moment of high expectations followed by embarrassing rejection?

"Then Samuel asked Jesse, "Is this it? Are there no more sons?"

"Well, yes, <u>there's</u> <u>the</u> <u>runt</u>. But he's out tending the sheep."

"Samuel ordered Jesse, "Go get him. We're not moving from this spot until he's here."

Jesse sent for him. He was brought in, the very picture of health—bright-eyed, good-looking. God said, "Up on your feet! Anoint him! This is the one."

Samuel took his flask of oil and anointed him, with his brothers standing around watching. The Spirit of God entered David like a rush of wind, God vitally empowering him for the rest of his life."[44]

In this account, we see that the family system held all the other brothers in high esteem. David was merely *the runt* sent out to tend sheep. He hadn't even been invited to sacrifice and worship. The image from his childhood in this account is not unusual in the world today. What about the older brothers? Samuel had to tell them to get on their feet for David's anointing. In a healthy family, there would be rejoicing because of this astounding news. It sounds as though this announcement did not bring unity to this family. That is proved out when David shows up on the battlefield where Goliath is tormenting the Israelite troops as recorded in 1 Samuel 17 in The Message.

"Goliath stood there and called out to the Israelite troops, "Why bother using your whole army? Am I not Philistine enough for you? And you're all committed to Saul, aren't you? So pick your best fighter and pit him against me. If he gets the upper hand and kills me, the Philistines will all become your slaves. But if I get the upper hand

---

[44] 1 Samuel 16:1-13, MSG

and kill him, you'll all become our slaves and serve us. I challenge the troops of Israel this day. Give me a man. Let us fight it out together!" When Saul and his troops heard the Philistine's challenge, they were terrified and lost all hope."

Jesse's three oldest sons were among these troops. We don't see them leading the charge to bring the bully giant down. As we read the rest of the account, it is important to see the exchange between David and his brother when he was standing at a turning point in his life.

"Enter David. One day, Jesse told David his son, "Take this sack of cracked wheat and these ten loaves of bread and run them down to your brothers in the camp. And take these ten wedges of cheese to the captain of their division. Check in on your brothers to see whether they are getting along all right, and let me know how they're doing—Saul and your brothers, and all the Israelites in their war with the Philistines in the Oak Valley."

David was up at the crack of dawn and, having arranged for someone to tend his flock, took the food and was on his way just as Jesse had directed him. He arrived at the camp just as the army was moving into battle formation, shouting the war cry. Israel and the Philistines moved into position, facing each other, battle-ready. David left his bundles of food in the care of a sentry, ran to the troops who were deployed, and greeted his brothers. While they were talking together, the Philistine champion, Goliath of Gath, stepped out from the front lines of the Philistines, and gave his usual challenge. David heard him.

The Israelites, to a man, fell back the moment they saw the giant—totally frightened. The talk among the troops was, "Have you ever seen anything like this, this man openly and defiantly challenging Israel? The man who kills the giant will have it made. The king will give him a huge reward, offer his daughter as a bride, and give his entire family a free ride."

David, who was talking to the men standing around him, asked, "What's in it for the man who kills that Philistine and gets rid of this ugly blot on Israel's honor? Who does he think he is, anyway, this uncircumcised Philistine, taunting the armies of God-Alive?"

They told him what everyone was saying about what the king would do for the man who killed the Philistine.

Eliab, his older brother, heard David fraternizing with the men and lost his temper: "What are you doing here! Why aren't you minding your own business, tending that scrawny flock of sheep? I know what you're up to. You've come down here to see the sights, hoping for a ringside seat at a bloody battle!"

"What is it with you?" replied David. "All I did was ask a question." Ignoring his brother, he turned to someone else, asked the same question, and got the same answer as before."

David did not let Eliab distract him. As we read what this older brother said to David, we get a sense of his total disdain and dislike for his little brother. Eliab was, in the family's eyes, the best of the best. He was supposed to get all the attention and honor. There may have been a family system in place to suppress the younger ones and "keep them in their place." Now David had been anointed to be the next king. Eliab couldn't stand the thought that he would also turn out to be a great warrior. His remarks about David were lies.

The Scripture tells how David had been obedient to his father, responsible, and reliable before he left the herd. We can feel the jealousy, the anger, and the sense of disappointment that Eliab had. It wasn't supposed to be this way. He was supposed to be the best.

David ignored him. David had confidence and knew who he was because he knew God was the source of his strength and courage. He wasn't going to take up the wrong battle. He turns to the purpose God had for him rather than letting reactive anger keep him from it.

"Master," said David, "don't give up hope. I'm ready to go and fight this Philistine."

Saul answered David, "You can't go and fight this Philistine. You're too young and inexperienced—and he's been at this fighting business since before you were born."

David said, "I've been a shepherd, tending sheep for my father. Whenever a lion or bear came and took a lamb from the flock, I'd go after it, knock it down, and rescue the lamb. If it turned on me, I'd grab it by the throat, wring its neck, and kill it. Lion or bear, it made no difference—I killed it. And I'll do the same to this Philistine pig who is taunting the troops of God-Alive. God, who delivered me from the teeth of the lion and the claws of the bear, will deliver me from this Philistine."

Saul said, "Go. And God help you!"

In this familiar story, we know the final outcome and see the results from staying focused on God and acknowledging that He gives us everything we need to succeed in whatever He has called us to do with our lives. In David's hand, which was empowered by God's strength and guided by His Spirit, one smooth stone landed the fatal blow that ended the enemy's tormenting reign over His people. Be sure you are fighting the right battle; the one God called you to fight will always produce the right results.

Wounded people around us do not have to be given the ability to distract us and diminish our lives. Schoolmates, co-workers, and even close friends leave unresolved soul wounds that fester in our hearts and can spew out in anger. David did what is so often very difficult for us to do. He ignored the comments. He knew who he was, so he knew none of his brother's words was true. It wasn't about him.

It was about Eliab being set up to be jealous of David because of a family system that told him he was the best. Eliab had never been loved and appreciated for who he was; perhaps he believed that if he wasn't the best, he was nothing. There is never a sense of identity in that shadowy world of having to earn love. In that world, we are only as valuable as the next great thing we must do. That is a genuine thing that happens today.

In fact, Eliab used the weapons that anger gives us so we can hide from our unhealed hurts. We see these weapons in the world and, sadly, in our homes today. He used *sarcasm* and *criticism* with lethal intent and deadly aim. He obviously wanted to hurt David and kill his confidence so he wouldn't do what Eliab couldn't do – find the courage to defeat the giant. When Eliab lost his "look good," he wanted to make David look bad.

The etymology of the word sarcasm is from the Greek word *sarkazein*, which means to 'tear flesh away.' That weapon lines up with what Jesus taught about anger. *"You're familiar with the command to the ancients, 'Do not murder.' I'm telling you that anyone who is so much as angry with a brother or sister is guilty of murder.* [45] John repeated that teaching, saying, *"Anyone who hates another brother or sister is really a murderer at heart."* [46]

When we hold on to the anger from past hurts, we direct it toward others on life's path with us. It will usually kill off the relationship. If the relationship does continue, we kill their identity, plant lies in their souls, and leave them feeling hopeless and alone.

But don't miss the sadness in this story over what Eliab is doing to himself. Who was he talking to? Not just his little brother — he was talking to the man who had been anointed to be his next king.

What did Eliab believe he was entitled to; what was his heart longing to hear spoken over him? Position, respect, hero-worship. He was talking to the very man who could have helped him attain all those things. David could have spoken those things to his brother.

God had gifted Eliab with strength, good looks, and leadership skills. But Eliab's anger spilled over and poisoned his opportunities, and he wasted his gifting. Searching Scriptures, there are no more mentions of Eliab, David's brother. Sadly, the king's oldest brother is not one of the named Mighty Men of Valor. Far too many men and

---

[45] Jesus' Sermon on the Mount, Matthew 5:21, MSG
[46] 1 John 3:15, NLT

women who have been called to the King have let unhealed soul wounds fester until they bubble out as anger and kill off all the "what might have been" in their lives.

David's family never said what the little boy David's soul longed to hear either. God was the one who had been teaching him and talking to him. It is only conjecture, but some of the things that happened later in David's life look like Lo-debar shadows. We can wonder if the fact that he looked for love in the wrong place and then desperately covered that sin up with a murder so he could still be seen as one of the "good guys" was in part because every child longs for parents and siblings who value them and let them know they are loved unconditionally. David may well have been a King with an orphan spirit hidden deep in his broken heart.

David didn't get affirmation from his family, and perhaps he never processed that hurt and heard God speak to his heart about how much he was loved and valued. He wrote Psalm 51 from his contrite and broken heart over his sin. It is a beautiful Psalm that is very familiar to those of us who have cried out for God to create a clean heart in us. Verse 6 speaks powerfully about the inner work that God calls us to do and perhaps sheds light on David's journey. *"Behold, You desire truth in the inward parts, and in the hidden part, You will make me to know wisdom."* David had come to understand that God will help us heal the lies-believed-as-truth stored in our souls and driving our beliefs; He will give us wisdom about our past. He wants to transform our understanding of our past so He can redeem our future.

There has never been a perfect family, and other than Jesus; there has never been a perfect person. Even Jesus' earthly family wasn't always supportive. Mark's gospel records, *"One time Jesus entered a house, and the crowds began to gather again. Soon he and his disciples couldn't even find time to eat. When his family heard what was happening, they tried to take him away. "He's out of his mind," they said."*[47]

Jesus knows first-hand what it is like when people say hurtful things. He is the one we can go to for healing those deep, lasting wounds. We find evidence that He healed the broken parts within his earthly family through the rest of His days of ministry. When I considered that the extraordinary Son of Man was placed in an ordinary family, I let myself imagine what it might have been like. These are some of my reflections, not Biblical teachings.

Since the tongue is the weapon of choice when anger is allowed to rule a person, to me, there is great significance that Jesus' brother James wrote powerful Truth about the use of our tongues.

The tongue is a small thing that makes grand speeches. But a tiny spark can set a great forest on fire. And among all the parts of the body, the tongue is a flame of fire. It is a whole world of wickedness, corrupting your entire body. It can set your whole life on fire, for it is set on fire by hell itself.

People can tame all kinds of animals, birds, reptiles, and fish, but no one can tame the tongue. It is restless and evil, full of

---

deadly poison. Sometimes it praises our Lord and Father, and sometimes it curses those who have been made in the image of God. And so blessing and cursing come pouring out of the same mouth. Surely, my brothers and sisters, this is not right!"[48]

James admits he understands that we can't tame our tongues. Only by submitting ourselves to God can we overcome the anger that rolls off our tongues all too easily when we have unhealed soul wounds. His verses also give insight into what some of Jesus' family may have felt.

"If you are wise and understand God's ways, prove it by living an honorable life, doing good works with the humility that comes from wisdom. But if you are bitterly jealous and there is selfish ambition in your heart, don't cover up the truth with boasting and lying. For jealousy and selfishness are not God's kind of wisdom. Such things are earthly, unspiritual, and demonic. For wherever there is jealousy and selfish ambition, there you will find disorder and evil of every kind.

But the wisdom from above is first of all pure. It is also peace-loving, gentle at all times, and willing to yield to others. It is full of mercy and the fruit of good deeds. It shows no favoritism and is always sincere. And those who are peacemakers will plant seeds of peace and reap a harvest of righteousness."[49]

James is so transparent here. Imagine with me what it was like to be Jesus' brother. Again, these are some of my reflections, not

---

[48] Description of the Tongue, James 3:5-10, NLT
[49] Root of Anger, James 3:14-18, NLT

Biblical teachings. There may have been some jealousy and envy. Who wouldn't want to walk on water, cast out demons, and feed thousands with a handful of fish and a few loaves of bread? It would be hard to shine in the world when your brother is the Light of Life.

Jesus didn't push him away, though, He worked on His relationship with His brother and taught him the things of Heaven. I believe James is describing Jesus in that last section. When we read that, we feel His presence. He brings peace to us when we give our hurt from harsh words to Him. Then, just like He did in James' life, He helps us become peacemakers in our world. Through Him, we can heal our hearts and souls; and our families, too.

Anger may also be masking pain caused by physical trauma that can cause many levels of pain. In Mephibosheth's life, trauma caused a physical limitation that lasted a lifetime. Accidents of all sorts leave behind lasting pain that started as physical pain but resulted in soul wounds. When there is no cure for physical limitation, the soul wounds can be made worse because it is an ongoing, daily situation of frustration. Sadly, our culture doesn't know how to respond to those among us who are physically different properly. Identity and worth are often seemingly diminished by the actions of those around us that foster the lie inside your soul that says you will never be who you could have been before this happened.

There is an old saying, *the saddest words of man are not what was, but what might have been.* However, there is Truth that says, *"You are God's masterpiece. He has created you anew in Christ*

*Jesus, so you **can do** the good things **He** planned for you long ago.*[50]

Our "what might have been" was probably a lesser dream than the one God has had for us all along. Larry Crabb, a revered Christian psychologist and Bible teacher, has journeyed with thousands through transformation. He wrote from a heart that has seen these words as true: "*There's never a moment in all our lives, from the day we trusted Christ till the day we see Him, when God is not longing to bless us. At every moment, in every circumstance, God is doing us good. He never stops. It gives Him too much pleasure. God is not waiting to bless us after our troubles end. He is blessing us right now, in and through those troubles.*[51]

If you are still on earth, God is not done with you. You may not have the same purpose you thought, but God's ways are higher than ours. Talk to Him about how He sees you now. Ask Him to give you dreams and visions about how you can be used in His kingdom now.

There was a woman I knew who grew up in a poor farming area during the Depression. Her parents were good people, but they had a daily struggle just to live through another day. When she was sixteen, they made her quit school because they couldn't buy shoes for her. Then they forced her into a marriage with a man who, in exchange for her, helped them out financially. All that young girl wanted was an education so she could better herself. Instead, she was

---

[50] Who You Are, Ephesians 2:10, NLT
[51] Larry Crabb, Shattered Dreams: God's Unexpected Path to Joy, Waterbrook Press, 2010

saddled with a very cruel man; she didn't get a voice or a vote in this horrific decision. When she was eighteen, she left the man, walked to a faraway big town, and found work. She ultimately divorced the man and set out to prove she was capable and worthy. She learned, worked hard, and "became somebody" in her world, remarried, and lived unhappily ever after.

She was angry and used that anger to set anyone around her straight if they didn't do things her way. When she was in the public eye, she could sometimes hold the anger at bay, releasing her rage when she got home. The anger didn't go away over time. The anger grew. She used alcohol to numb the pain and soothe the rage. Over time the use of that increased as well. She had accomplished every single thing she had set out to do. With each achieved goal, she found only the emptiness and pain she had been determined to overcome.

One by one, people distanced themselves. She had many acquaintances, yet no close, intimate friends. Three short years before her life on earth ended, she finally cried out to the God who had never given up on her. Year after year after year, He stood there, His heart and hands filled with all the blessings of Heaven, just waiting for her to turn to Him. She found peace during those last years, but she often said, "I wish I had known Him sooner; I'm so sorry I made it all so hard." She lives with Him now and knows He loves her. She has heard Him tell her how very strong that love is. She has also heard Him tell her how smart, creative, and unique He sees her and how much He values her.

Her parents' ill-advised actions out there in her Lo-debar

caused the darkness that settled in her soul. However, she was the one who gave the pain from her first eighteen years the power to overshadow her sixty remaining years. She left a legacy of brokenness and scorched hearts. The power for her to live a true and vibrant life was right there, wanting to transform her darkness. He is still right here today for each of us.

When anger continues to cover up the hurt, it is like picking at a scab on your knee. You may have an incident that causes you to take a quick peek back at the wound, but the anger helps you turn away to avoid dealing with it. Over time the scab becomes thicker and harder. It becomes so hardened that it seems impossible to face what really hurts. When it is impossible for you, it falls into the category of *Him-possible.*

Pour out the pain to God. He has not been caught off guard by what happened to you. You are not living out "Plan B." Let Him heal the pain, answer your hard questions, and tell you who you really are so He can reveal the amazing plan He has to use you in His kingdom now. He's been waiting for you to bring this to Him so it can be healed. He gets no greater joy than from blessing us simply because He loves us all so much. Let him heal the pain and take away the anger so He can give you blessings in exchange.

If your anger is directed at God, the most important thing that can happen in your life is for you to get honest and transparent with God about why you are so angry with Him. Genuinely seek out a godly minister who can give you a safe place to pour this out. Writing a letter to God is often where you can begin this process. Identify the root of the pain so you can look at the reason for the anger. He already knows, but this is an exercise for your soul.

Are you like Eliab? Did you think you were destined for a specific role, and then it didn't happen? Were you passed over? Why would God allow that? Ask Him, and be willing to truly listen for His answer. Did you serve in a war-torn country and come out with deep hurts and maybe physical challenges? Was the living room of your home a battleground? Where was God? Why didn't He stop it? Did you lose a loved one, and the grief is so oppressive that you feel like you can't breathe? He will understand! He had to turn away from his own dying son when our sin was laid on Him. Please let Him talk to you about your pain. The anger inside you has gone on long enough. Angry tongues, either yours or others, have set enough of your life on fire. Tell hell, "No more!" Let Jesus set you back on the path He has for you.

Words kill, words give life; they're either poison or fruit; you choose.[52] When we know Jesus, we know life for the first time. Life itself creates a desire for more life. He said He came to give us life more abundantly. There is only one who came to steal, kill, and destroy. Being a born-again Christian, we now have a choice about who we will follow. No matter how painful your past was or how difficult your current situation is, there is a way for you to move out of the effects of all that and claim the life you were created to live.

Reach out to Jesus, and ask Him to show you the Words for

---

[52] Proverbs 18:21, MSG

you to speak to claim that life. Reach out to others in the faith. James called us his brothers and sisters in the faith because we are. You have a bigger family than you can even imagine. Many of us are still working on healing and transformation and learning how to live differently, too. Come, join in, and find your place among us. None of us are interested in religion, but we love learning to hear from our Father. We are growing in ways to encourage and relate to each other. Come, listen for the Words your soul has longed to hear for far too long.

דְּרוֹר

Chapter Ten

Fighting From Victory

Mephibosheth lost his father in an earthly battle during a war that had been raging for years. The aftermath of that battle plunged him into a chaotic environment of lack, lies, limitations, and silenced Truth. Many of us have lived in that same place.

When Our Father calls us to Him, we are born anew. Everything in us begins to awaken, and our Spirit now speaks Transformation and Truth. Unfortunately, another war has been raging for eons, and the leader of the ongoing battles there will work against our new life. The devil wants to do everything he can to keep us from becoming everything we are meant to be.

Unknowingly, we entered a raging battle for control over our lives while on Earth. This battle cannot kill us because Our Savior defeated death so that we will live eternally in Heaven.[53] It is not a battle that can derail us from entering God's Kingdom because He has called us to be His children. The devil can't win the war because Jesus already has won the Victory. He also won our souls to Him. We are His, and He is ours.

It is essential, however, to recognize that we are in a battle to keep us from advancing God's kingdom on Earth. So, we must know the tactics of our enemy. Even the ancient Taoist Sun Tzu, the great

---

[53] Death is Overcome, 1 Corinthians 15:50-58, NLT

military strategist, understood this wisdom. In his book, *The Art of War*, he wrote, *"Know thy enemy and know yourself; in a hundred battles, you will never be defeated. When you are ignorant of the enemy but know yourself, your chances of winning or losing are equal. If ignorant both of your enemy and of yourself, you are sure to be defeated in every battle."* [54] Football coaches specialize in this idea and have their team relentlessly train and learn their plays, but then they turn their attention to the opposing team's game films. They look for weaknesses and use them to win.   It is essential to know your opponent.

In the very season of our life when we are seeking our True Identity, the enemy of our soul will launch his greatest attack. The focus of his vile attack is to prevent us from knowing who we really are in Christ. That serpentine whisperer of lies knows better than we do where our power, our effectiveness, and even our very lives are found.

While we keep pressing in to hear Our Father tell us who we are, we also need to learn the tactics of our enemy.

When we come to faith in Jesus out of Lo-debar, our "normal" doesn't adjust immediately to Kingdom normal. Think about this from the perspective of the Israelites when they had been in the wilderness and finally made it to the edge of the Promised Land. Moses sent twelve spies to see this Promised Land so they could know their enemy and have an effective plan to defeat them.

---

[54] Art of War, Sun Tzu, public domain

Ten of the twelve spread "evil reports" about the land. How could they do that? Was it what their time in bondage had stored in their heart? Did they want to be their own God? Did they want to decide between good and evil? Only two, Joshua and Caleb, "turned their eyes to God." When they looked for God's Truth, they saw the abundance. *"We went into the land to which you sent us, and it does flow with milk and honey! Here is its fruit."*[55] Ten of them saw only the mission's obstacles, challenges, and impossibility.

The ten used some of the most powerful weapons the devil had formed for them while they were in the wilderness. As soon as Moses had led them out of their captivity, they began to "murmur," or as we say today, they started to complain. Soon, it became their "normal" for how they lived. Their focus was on the problem they faced, not the power of their God. They used their **negativity** and **words of complaint** to impact the *entire group of people*. The Apostle Paul uses the ten to illustrate the lessons we glean while studying the Israelites' wilderness journey. He says, *"Don't complain, as some of them also complained and were destroyed by the destroyer."*[56] Relationships, businesses, opportunities, potential, possibilities, and health can all be diminished or destroyed by these two evil-formed tools. These two are proven blessing blockers in our lives. They, indeed, were effective that day at the door to the blessings God had promised them.

Were they so negative because God gave them a blessing that didn't meet their expectations? We do that sometimes. We think that

---

[55] The Scouting Report, Numbers 13 and 14, NLT
[56] 1 Cor., Chapter 10:10, NLT

God's blessings will float down from Heaven and require nothing from us; it should be easy if it is from God, right? Let's look back at the beginning. If we go back to the first Paradise He created for His creations, we find this, *"Then the Lord God took the man and put him in the garden of Eden to tend and keep it."* When He created Eve, He said, *"I will make him a helper comparable to him."*[57] All the gardeners reading this will deeply understand what it means to "tend and keep" a garden. It is a great deal of work.

Somehow, mankind has journeyed to a place where people think work is a "four-letter word." Working with God and others is a great honor and deeply satisfying. However, the enemy of our soul has distorted this as he has so many things.

Two of the spies believed in God's faithfulness enough to go forward. They saw the obvious challenges but knew God always works with us to fulfill His promises through His power. Each of us must answer this breakthrough question: *Do I really want this life that my Father has for me badly enough to believe and join my Savior in the battle for my identity?* When we answer yes, we fix our eyes on Jesus as we consider the weapons of our enemy.

What comes to your mind when you think of the devil? Red critter with horns, pointed ears, barbed tail, an evil sneer on his face, or perhaps a serpent slithering about? The comic images in the world around us might very well be tactics to throw us off. We must look to Scripture to see an accurate description. We don't want to miss the

---

[57] God creates Adam and Eve, Genesis 2, NKJV

point that God described him for us in great detail.[58] He wants us to be prepared.

"You were the model of perfection, full of wisdom and exquisite in beauty. You were in Eden, the garden of God. Your clothing was adorned with every precious stone all beautifully crafted for you and set in the finest gold. They were given to you on the day you were created. I ordained and anointed you as the mighty angelic guardian. You had access to the holy mountain of God and walked among the stones of fire. You were blameless in all you did from the day you were created until the day evil was found in you.

For you said to yourself, 'I will ascend to heaven and set my throne above God's stars.

I will preside on the mountain of the gods far away in the north. I will climb to the highest heavens and be like the Most High.'"

The enemy of our soul was a beautiful creature; he walked with God. He knows God's ways, the allure of beautiful earthly things, and how the people God puts in charge of children are supposed to be "angelic guardians." He also has an agenda. The devil wants to become *The Most High*. He uses all he knows about God as weapons to keep us from God. This vile critter will not be satisfied with a little bit of our lives; he wants to reign supreme in our lives.

He can't kill us because Jesus has already defeated death. Jesus has taken the power out of all the generational curses agreed upon over us at the gates of hell, so we are released from those.

---

[58] Descriptions of Lucifer, Taken from the Ezekiel 25 and Isaiah 14:13-14, NLT

Neither can he separate us from God's love. The promises of God are True, and He said to us,

"Can anything ever separate us from Christ's love? Does it mean he no longer loves us if we have trouble or calamity, or are persecuted, or hungry, or destitute, or in danger, or threatened with death? No, despite all these things, overwhelming victory is ours through Christ, who loved us.

And I am convinced that nothing can ever separate us from God's love. Neither death nor life, neither angels nor demons, neither our fears for today nor our worries about tomorrow—not even the powers of hell can separate us from God's love. No power in the sky above or in the earth below—indeed, nothing in all creation will ever be able to separate us from the love of God that is revealed in Christ Jesus our Lord."[59]

All the maneuvers of the devil are plans to limit our understanding of who we are so that we can't be a force for God to advance His Kingdom on earth. As believers reaching for transformation, we can almost hear his vile words echoing from Eden, *"Did God really say that. .?"* So many of us never heard the things our souls hungered for spoken by our earthly parents. Because of that, we can be easily led to doubt what our heavenly Father has said to us today.

The ten spies knew the power, provision, and presence of God in their daily walk; however, they let God diminish in their Spiritual

---

[59] The Apostle Paul's message from God to Roman Believers, Romans 8:35: 37-39, NLT

eyes because of what they saw with their natural eyes. When they forgot what He had done in their past, they missed what He wanted to do in their future. They were diverted from the plan God had for them. That is what the devil wants us to do today.

As we dig into the strategies of the enemy of our soul, we must remain prayerful so that we stay aware that Jesus is right there with us. If there is a reaction in our soul, we may need to stop and spend time with Him about what came up at that point.

Tactics – Weapons Formed Against Us

The Knowledge of Evil

In the beginning of life on earth, God warned against tasting the fruit of the tree of the knowledge of good and evil. When we have walked through trauma, there is a part of our soul that deeply wishes we had never come to have the knowledge of evil. However, when we have seen evil acts, we can never un-see them. When we have heard evil, cruel things spoken, we can never un-hear them. When we have carried out evil acts ourselves, we can never un-know that we did them. We never walk away from knowing we are capable of evil, that evil hurts us, and others around us, and that evil may be just around the corner.

The devil and his demons perpetuate evil to keep us from having a deep knowledge of Good. Be aware of the effects of your past because the enemy wants to keep you bound to it. He, too, is like that football coach who studies game films of the opponents. He has reviewed our lives, and when we step forward in salvation and move toward transformation, he will play back the evil in our lives and turn it into evidence to prove we are unlovable and incapable of receiving God's love.

He may remind you of the evil and blame God for it. You may be dealing with this if you hear things like, *If God loved you, why did He let that happen? You are damaged goods; no one will be able to see past your scars to truly love you. Remember when you did that? God will never let you into His Heaven because you are too evil.*

He may also send other people to bring you his vile message. Maybe you did do evil things before you knew Jesus and lived in a land where evil was normal. Those are things **you did, not who you are**. You are a new creation, forgiven because of Jesus' sacrifice. As we discussed in the forgiveness chapter, we are told to confess the sin, turn away from doing that ever again, and then go and ask forgiveness from the one we harmed with a willing heart to make amends. If you have done that, you stand pure and blameless before the Lord. You are a new creation!!

"When God our Savior revealed his kindness and love, He saved us, not because of the righteous things we had done, but because of his mercy. He washed away our sins, giving us a new birth and new life through the Holy Spirit. He generously poured out the Spirit upon us through Jesus Christ, our Savior. Because of his grace, he made us right in his sight and gave us confidence that we will inherit eternal life."[60]

No matter what you have done, Jesus washed it away! You

---

[60] Meaning of Born Again, Titus 3:5, NLT

are not evil. If you hear that from somewhere in your soul, stomp your foot and tell the devil to shut up!

Sometimes, however, if you hurt a non-believer or a demonized believer, they may be under the influence of demons and still hate and accuse the old person you were. They may want to persecute and revile you and blame you for all the bad in their life. Pray for their deliverance. Pray for wisdom from God as to how to handle this. Ask God to help you love them with a healthy love and see them the way He sees them.

Jesus walked away from His accusers, and you may need to set boundaries in your life so you aren't a target for their venom. Boundaries are used to keep the Life that Jesus has given you safe.

Every time Jesus encountered a demonized person, the demons immediately recognized Him. If you have a person like this in your life and you have to be in their presence, be sure to go in the position of these three things; Pray for a clean heart where they are concerned, ask your trusted mentors and prayer warriors to cover you in prayer, and let the Light and Love of Jesus fill you up and flow out of you. That person needs Him, and by carrying His Spirit, you may be a force for deliverance for them. When the demons faced Jesus, they cried out for mercy and rolled over. Pray that happens for this person.

Your knowledge of the evil you did in the past may also be used to cast a shadow on the joy that should be yours. Combat warriors often carry false guilt because of the bloody battles they had to fight so evil could be pushed back. The battle was against evil ideologies and greed of a country's leaders, but it was carried out in flesh and blood.

The enemy wants to accuse and condemn you for carrying out military orders. That is what evil does. Come together with others who have survived this type of evil for support and encouragement, but also take it to Jesus. He is a man of sorrows. He knows what it is like to see the wages of sin and war; He cried over Jerusalem because He saw the battle that was coming.

"But as he came closer to Jerusalem and saw the city ahead, he began to weep. "How I wish today that you, of all people, would understand the way to peace. But now it is too late, and peace is hidden from your eyes. Before long, your enemies will build ramparts against your walls and encircle you and close in on you from every side. They will crush you into the ground, and your children with you. Your enemies will not leave a single stone in place, because you did not recognize it when God visited you."[61]

The word translated as "weep" means a sudden grip of deep sorrow that triggers an outcry. Your Savior knows the evil you walked in during the war, and you can talk to Him about it. Tell Him what you saw and felt and hated about it all. He knows, and He doesn't want you to let it fester in the dark – that is where the enemy of your soul can store it away and torment you with it. Bring it to His Light, and He will heal it and set you Free. You walked as a valiant warrior on the earth; imagine how powerful you can be in the Lord's Army.

---

[61] Jesus entered Jerusalem, Luke 19:41-44, NLT

Don't let satan rob you of that honor and joy. You and your message and strength can advance Good in the world, which will help defeat evil forces. Once you are born again, you are a child of His kingdom. Evil doesn't live around you and through you. The demons want to continue to make you believe you are always subject to evil. That is a vile lie straight from the devil's forked tongue.

Weapons of Mass Distractions

The enemy also has "weapons of mass *distractions*" to use against us. We must be alert to what he is throwing at us, so we can be intentional about how we live our lives. These weapons show up in a variety of ways.

Remember, in the description of Lucifer, we read that he was given many jewels set in gold. He has used that knowledge to distract us by having us think that life is nothing more than the pursuit of things. *If we can just get a house in that neighborhood, we will be happy. If I just made more money, I would be happy. etc., etc.* Often our desire for things will lead us into debt and depression. The new car smell will still be lingering when we see the latest model of cars come out, causing the thought, *Ooh, I want one of those.* This is a distraction to keep us from the joy that God has for us when we allow Him to transform us into the person He means for us to be. He is our only source of Joy.

This distraction takes many forms. We can keep our families busy running after all the "right" earthly stuff. The right neighborhood, the right schools and cheer teams, and sports teams, the right designer names to wear. We may even need to be at the "right" church to fit in with the culture. When we are looking for all the "right" things to make us happy, we are on the wrong path, one that will lead to the destruction of our relationship with the only one who can bring us Joy and give us Life.

In this battle for our identity, the enemy then launches the weapon of discontentment. When we strive and work and scramble to get all those things, and we don't have the happiness we thought we would have, we are discontent with the things and also with the people with us as we acquire them. Thoughts like, *If my wife were more outgoing, we would be happier with the neighborhood. If my husband didn't work all the time, we wouldn't be having this problem. My kids never win the awards, even after all the money we spent on lessons.* The enemy is sly about this and sometimes just turns it inward. Then we think, *I guess people just don't like me.*

Distractions are often launched from many platforms. Social media, pop-up ads, and breaking news can all keep us distracted. We seek to be entertained and get bombarded with "marketing ploys" to pull us away from our lives. Measure your screen time and see how it is divided. Do we spend more time on Wordle than we do in His Word? Are TikTok influencers robbing you of your purpose to influence the world for God as the minutes of your life tick away? Where are you turning your thoughts each day?

We have a Savior who loves us, who cries over us, who bleeds for us, and whose heart desires to be closer to each of us. How much attention do we give Him each day?

When stuff, position, and personal achievements become the

center of our life, it will always disappoint us. The enemy knows that and uses it to keep us from the One who never will disappoint. If your first waking thought and last reflection at night are on this stuff, be aware that you have become distracted from the important things of True life.

Divide and Conquer

The United States of America was established with a focus on being free. We still have more freedom than other countries, but what good has it done us? Look at the degrading, demeaning posts on any social platform today, and your heart will break. There are no intelligent discussions about important topics; instead, there are agendas, anger, and anti-everything.

These words of the Apostle Paul are wisdom for us all to remember,

"For you have been called to live in freedom, my brothers and sisters. But don't use your freedom to satisfy your sinful nature. Instead, use your freedom to serve one another in love. For the whole law can be summed up in this one command: "Love your neighbor as yourself." But, if you are always biting and devouring one another, watch out! Beware of destroying one another."[62]

Beware, indeed. Proverbs 12 states it another way, *"But he who hates correction is stupid."*

The greatest, most effective tool the devil has is to bring division. Schools were begun in America because the Puritans

---

[62] Galatians 5:13-15, NLT

supported literacy *so people could read the Bible.* How many families today are letting school boards, who refuse to let the Bible even be mentioned, set the moral standards for the children God has entrusted to parents? Children are being turned away from their parents.

Recent years have brought many mass casualties, 9/11, COVID, and mass shootings across our country, often costing the lives of innocent young children. With each traumatic event, we come together as a country, speak unity and strength, and pledge to stop these things. While the nation's roaring chant, *U-S-A! U-S-A!* is still echoing across our land; the enemy comes in and turns us all against each other so that we sink lower into the abyss of division.

Perhaps the root of this is the division within the church. Denominational pride, divisive people, and rigid religiousness have stymied the growth of many churches and have been the sad end of some. When His Bride is divided, she can't be the force for unity that the world needs.

Jesus stands at the right hand of Our Father, making intercession for us all. I sometimes sense He is praying what He prayed while He was still on earth, *"I am praying not only for these disciples but also for all who will ever believe in me through their message. I pray that they will all be one, just as you and I are one— as you are in me, Father, and I am in you. And may they be in us so that the world will believe you sent me.* [63]

Let's not be stupid!

---

[63] John 17:20-21, NLT

In Lo-debar, we can establish an appetite for sin. Without an identity, or a shepherd, many things that seemed "right" and "normal" out there were neither. The time spent there, however, may have created an appetite in our soul for that sin. A difficult passage in Exodus tells us God said,

"The Lord, the Lord God, merciful and gracious,

longsuffering, and abounding in goodness

and truth, keeping mercy for thousands, forgiving iniquity

and transgression and sin, by no means clearing the

guilty, visiting the iniquity of the fathers upon the children

and the children's children to the third and the fourth

generation."[64]

If God forgives the sin and iniquity, why is it visited upon the future generations? We must notice that He doesn't say *He punishes* the future generations for their parents' sins. But when there is sin in a family, children learn to consider that sin is an option for their life..

Some people will tell a lie when many times, it would have been better to tell the truth. Lying may have been modeled in their household as a way to give an excuse, avoid responsibility, or make oneself look good. It seems normal. It seems to be the right way to handle situations. It is neither. Once we are born again, Jesus creates a desire in our hearts for the righteousness of the kingdom. That would include radical honesty in all our dealings with people. The

---

[64] God speaks to Moses, Exodus 34:6-7, NKJV

enemy will use that weakness from your past to perpetuate the sin of lying, sometimes to the point of lying to yourself about the fact that you tell lies. We call them excuses or dress them up with cute names, "little white lies," or "fibs."

Suppose our first sexual encounters were carried out secretly to hide from parents or peers. That can create an unnatural appetite for illicit sex because of the adrenaline rush that comes from the need for secrecy. Later, that can lead to an affair, and once it is discovered, the appetite for secrecy goes away, and the affair ends. Usually, however, this will be repeated because the iniquity created an appetite for secret, illicit sex.

There are many sins that fall into this category. Understanding the root of persistent sin helps us rid it from our lives. If you grew up in a family where the use of alcohol was prevalent, there is a greater chance that you struggle with addiction to alcohol. Maybe you drank to fit in. You wanted to hear that you were one of the guys, so your behavior followed. Perhaps your parents unwisely spent money to fit in with others. When you see that happen, it becomes normal. It's "what people do." You may be unable to handle your finances well. Was the talk in your family always gossip about others, perhaps filled with prejudices and slander? Is that iniquity coming down through you to your future generations, and it feels so "normal" and "right" that you don't even notice it?

Most Christians know the "Fruit of the Spirit" in Galatians 5:22-23. But if we are struggling to get free from the iniquities of our past, it is very important to read the results of our sinful nature listed in the prior verses. The Message Bible translates them into today's language; *"repetitive, loveless, cheap sex; a stinking accumulation of mental and emotional garbage; frenzied and joyless grabs for happiness; trinket gods; magic-show religion; paranoid loneliness; cutthroat competition; all-consuming-yet-never-satisfied wants; a brutal temper; an impotence to love or be loved; divided homes and divided lives; small-minded and lopsided pursuits; the vicious habit of depersonalizing everyone into a rival; uncontrolled and uncontrollable addictions; ugly parodies of community."[65]* The enemy of our soul looks back on our past, finds the weaknesses created there, and uses them to lure us back into the old thought patterns and actions so we will never yield the fruit of the Spirit. We must be watchful so we don't get dragged back into it.

Jesus will give us the strength and wisdom to destroy the sin before the sin destroys us.

Now that we have looked at some of the tactics, we must look at who we are up against. Who are these demons? They are the angels who sided with Lucifer and fell from Heaven with him. God cast him to the earth, and they followed. One-third of the angels were in this group. Fourteen demons are named in Scripture, and it is helpful to take a brief look at who they are and where they may show up in your life to rob you of all God wants for you. Some, like the religious spirit that comes to give a false sense of self-righteousness and keep believers from having a close relationship with God, and often

---

[65] The works of Selfish Desires, Galatians 5:19-21, MSG

distanced from other people, are very active but are not specifically named in Scripture.

This is not a comprehensive list of all evil spirits; it is just the ones I have found *named* in Scripture.

Spirit of Fear

This is probably the most misunderstood of the scriptures dealing with spiritual warfare. Most Christians take this out of context and use it as a catchall reminder to "fear not" many things. The *spirit of fear* is the demon that comes to hold us back and keep us from using the gifts, talents, abilities, and anointing to do Kingdom work. 2 Timothy 1:7 is the cited Scripture, but it begins with *"Therefore"* so we must always look to the preceding verse to understand what it is "there for."

Paul writes to Timothy, *"I remember your genuine faith, for you share the faith that first filled your grandmother Lois and your mother, Eunice. And I know that same faith continues strong in you. This is why I remind you to fan into flames the spiritual gift God gave you when I laid my hands on you. For God has not given us a spirit of fear and timidity but of power, love, and self-discipline."*

When Jesus announced His ministry, He read from the Scroll of Isaiah saying, *"The Spirit of the Sovereign Lord is upon me, for the Lord has anointed me to. . .*[66] He then read what the Lord had sent Him to do. As a follower of Jesus, we must press in and find our mission that He has given us. When we are clear, He will fan it into

---

[66] Jesus declares His Mission, Luke 4:18, NKJV

flames, and we will never need to be afraid of stepping into that role. This demon will do all he can to keep you from it. He screams to our soul that we aren't called as he tries to drown out the words of Our Savior, *"Come, Follow Me, and I will make you fishers of men and women."*

Spirit of Perverseness

An abundance of work is being accomplished in our culture today under the leadership of this demon. This spirit twists Truth, tells people they can do whatever they want, and then gives them a twisted way to justify what they have done. It is very seductive and targets young people.[67]

Spirit of Deaf and Dumbness

This does not mean physical deafness. Jesus referred to spiritual deafness by saying, *"Let those with ears to hear, hear."* If you can't hear God, it may be because this vile demon is trying to keep you from living the life Jesus wants you to live. Press into a time of deep prayer and fasting, tell Him you can't hear him, and tell Him how much you want to. This demon works hard to keep you from hearing God. Rebuke him and tell him he must go because you are a temple of the Holy Spirit, and he is forbidden from being in your life. [68]

Spirit of Lying

This demon wants to take up residence in your life, so the Holy Spirit, who is the Spirit of Truth, is edged out. The Lord used this

---

[67] Definition of the spirit of perverseness, Isaiah 19:14, NLT
[68] Jesus encounters the deaf and dumb spirit, Mark 9:25-27, NLT

demon to lead King Ahab into a doomed battle. We can allow this spirit into our lives when we don't bring the lies we have believed as our truth to Our Lord so He can speak Truth to us to replace them.[69]

Spirit of Heaviness

God knows we mourn. There is an entire book called Lamentations that allows for the mourning of Israel. But, when it is time, He wants to lift the heaviness off and restore our heavenly blessings. Healing the hurts from Lo-debar experiences is a very important part of mourning our past. *"To console those who mourn in Zion, To give them beauty for ashes, The oil of joy for mourning, The garment of praise for the spirit of heaviness."*[70]

Spirit of Error

This is closely related to the spirit of perversion, but it relates to religious beliefs. It can cause false doctrines and twisted truths from Scripture. It wants to lead people to major errors that cause them deep regret later.[71]

Spirit of Jealousy

This demon causes possessiveness and competition and can trigger hatred toward others. It is active in marriages to cause suspicion and division, but it can be rooted in the way children are treated by parents who show favoritism. It is one of the workings of the flesh found in Ephesians 5:2. The devil hates the unity of marriage, so we must all be alert to suspicious thoughts so there is no division.

---

[69] The spirit of lying, 2 Chronicles 18:22, NLT
[70] Isaiah 61:3, NKJV
[71] Mention of the spirit of error, 1 John 4:6, NLT

Spirit of Stupor

This demon is present when we numb our hearts so we do not hear and come to believe in God. It can come because we experienced hurt from people in the church who were hurt individuals themselves. If we judge God because of the actions of men, we can invite this spirit in. It is closely tied to the antichrist spirit. God used this spirit when some Israelites saw the miracles, heard Jesus' teachings, and refused to accept the gospel. *God has put them into a deep sleep. To this day he has shut their eyes so they do not see, and closed their ears so they do not hear."*[72]

Spirit of Antichrist

Satan's favorite demon, this one's name defines its work. It is against everything about Jesus, tries to keep us from Him, and seeks to discredit Our Lord. John warned us with these words, *"Dear friends, do not believe every spirit, but test the spirits to see whether they are from God, because many false prophets have gone out into the world."*[73] This vile creature is at work in the churches. Both the buildings where we worship and through the airways on mobile devices in the hands of believers around the world. How can we test the spirits? John continues, *"But if someone claims to be a prophet and does not acknowledge the truth about Jesus, that person is not from God. Such a person has the spirit of the Antichrist, which you heard is coming into the world and indeed is already here."*[74]

---

[72] Signs and Wonders Discounted, Romans 11:8, NLT
[73] 1 John 4:1-3, NKJV
[74] Warnings about the presence of the antichrist, 1 John 4:1, 3, NLT

When we are unaware of this demon, we will believe every engaging speaker and accept worldviews that are traps to keep us bound, so we become distant from Jesus. It will also keep us from "being fed" even when we hear a message through God's anointed. This also shows up on Sunday morning when a powerful word has been delivered and heard, but a couple may end up in a huge argument even before they get off the parking lot. He wants to keep us all from advancing in our relationships with Jesus and each other.

Spirit of Haughtiness

The devil is the perfect model for this demon. It brings an arrogant, prideful attitude and rejects God and any earthly authority figures.

Spirit of Whoredoms

This demon promotes a total lack of faithfulness of any kind, chronic dissatisfaction, excessive appetites, and a love of worldliness. The book of Hosea addresses the outcome when believers are not aware of the works of this demon.

Spirit of Infirmity

This demon does not seek to bring one illness on a person; it seeks to cause a lifetime of illness, physical weakness, and disorders. It works in opposition to the health and healing Jesus has for our lives.

Spirit of Bondage

This demon comes in through the indulgence of fleshly desires. It works to trap us in addictions of all types, including, but not limited to, alcohol, drugs, sex, and food. This is especially effective if a young child is introduced to things like alcohol and sex too soon. They do not have the reasoning ability to know it is wrong. It also can use fear of dying to keep us from the joy of living as Christ's followers.

Spirit of Divination

This causes a desire to be able to tell the future by supernatural means and to be able to read significance into events by summoning up spirits to explain them. God wants to reveal all the mysterious things to us if we will just call to Him and ask. He is the only One Who truly knows.

Whew, so now we have looked at the ways of the enemy and the missions of some of his demons. We look at this so we will stay alert to demonic work. There is much more in Scripture for you to find if you got prompted about a certain area. Jesus is always with you to talk to about this.

What does Scripture tell us about this battle raging around us while we seek to hear Our Father say who we are to Him? What is our strategy?

"Stay alert! Watch out for your great enemy, the devil. He prowls around like a roaring lion, looking for someone to devour. Stand firm against him, and be strong in your faith.

Since we have been made right in God's sight by faith, we have peace with God because of what Jesus Christ our Lord has done for us. Because of our faith, Christ has brought us into this place of undeserved privilege where we now stand, and we confidently and joyfully look forward to sharing God's glory.

*A final word: Be strong in the Lord and **in his mighty power**. Put on all of God's armor so that you will be able to stand firm against all strategies of the devil. For we are not fighting against flesh-and-blood enemies, but against evil rulers and authorities of the unseen world, against mighty powers in this dark world, and against evil spirits in the heavenly places.*

*Therefore, put on **every piece** of God's armor so you will be able to resist the enemy in the time of evil. Then after the battle you will still be standing firm. Stand your ground, putting on the belt of truth and the body armor of God's righteousness. For shoes, put on the peace that comes from the Good News so that you will be fully prepared. In addition to all of these, hold up the shield of faith to stop the fiery arrows of the devil. Put on salvation as your helmet, and take the sword of the Spirit, which is the word of God.*

Pray in the Spirit at all times and on every occasion. Stay alert and be persistent in your prayers for all believers everywhere. "[75]

We are instructed to stand firmly planted where God has placed us. He is with us. We aren't to fight in our own strength; our part is to believe in His faithfulness that will bring us through whatever the enemy can throw at us. We are being equipped and prepared to be in The Lord's Army and wear his Armor, never losing sight that we are all in this together.

We can't strap on a belt of Truth while we still believe the lies the devil has told us about ourselves, our God, and other people. We

---

[75] Apostle Paul's instructions for Victory over evil, Ephesians 6, NLT

can't put on a breastplate of righteousness while we are walking in the muck and mire of sin in our lives. There is no way to walk around in peace if we still hold anger, bitterness, and unforgiveness. We have no shield against the devil's attack when we have more faith in the power of our current situation to hold us back than we have in Our Savior to deliver us out of it. Our thoughts must be filled with the knowledge that we are saved from all this when we have given our lives to Christ. He is there with His written word and His Rhema word to communicate with us at all times.

Our basic training is to stand against the devil and call on the name of Jesus. Claim His authority; He gave it to us to use against them. Claim His power. Cast off any demons by commanding them to leave your life. Then bind them and command them not to return. Believe and declare that they have no right to your life and have no lasting effects on your circumstances. Proclaim the Truth and confess you know it, and believe it. Bind Truth in your heart by meditating on the words Jesus gives you.

This is a suggested format for prayer to help you get started.

"In the name of Jesus, I take His Authority over any demon; through His power, I bind you and cast you out of my life. You must now leave and go to the place Jesus prepared for you. You are not to return. Any effects of your attempt to defeat me are being redeemed by the blood of Jesus and being changed from curses into blessings. Holy Spirit, will you open up the storehouse of Heaven and pour out every good thing God has for me now?! Thank you, Father, You are the Father of Light, and I am grateful that You called me to be your child." Amen

So, let's leave the darkness behind, being sure that we have these takeaways with us:

- The enemy and all his demons have been defeated. If we still see the effects of darkness in our lives, it is because we have an open door and invite demons into our world. That is why we are pleading with all believers to be willing to get with Our Lord and open ourselves up to healing. Let's put an end to the lies, labels, and limitations from our "normal" past and step into the freedom that Jesus won for us the day He went to the cross for us.

- We cannot fight for our life, our marriage, our family, our career, or our calling with the weapons the enemy of our soul formed and used to try to defeat us. Identify the weapons you have been using. Do you use anger, sarcasm, criticism, condemnation, complaining, lies, or control? Do you use distractions like social media, endless tv, alcohol or other substances, or pornography to numb yourself and detach from problems? Do you let shame and guilt from your unconfessed sin keep you stuck rather than confessing and getting free so you can live? Invite Holy Spirit to show you what weapons you are using that are destroying rather than building up your life. Set them down outside the door you have left open to satan, slam that door shut, and leave them behind.

- May we all *KNOW* the enormity of Our God and join the Apostle Paul in this attitude, "*When we think of all this, we fall to our knees and pray to the Father, the Creator of everything in heaven and on earth. We pray that from His glorious, unlimited resources, He will empower us with inner strength through His Spirit. Then Christ will make His home in our hearts as we trust in Him. May our roots grow down into God's love and keep us strong. And may we have the power to understand, as all God's people should, how wide, how long, how high, and how deep His love is. May we experience the love of Christ, though it is too great to understand fully. Then we will be made complete with all the fullness of life and power that comes from God."[76]*

---

[76] Ephesians 3:14-19, NLT

דְּרוֹר

Chapter Eleven

Leaving Lo-debar

Are you ready? As John and I prayed over the content of this book, we wanted the work in this section to give you a sense of newness and renewed hope for what is coming next in your life. We also hope that some come to life in a new, more vibrant way. When I began to get free, everything seemed more full of light than before when everything seemed shadowy.

I created a section at the end of the book for taking possession of what God has planned for you. There are tools to help you continue working on any shadowy things that may arise. Remember, there can be many layers, and that nasty enemy always looks for the next opportune time. When a shadow from your past falls on your life, the guides in that section will help you talk with your Savior. He is always near to shed His Light.

My freedom process took years, and I am grateful for every moment. I was drawn in by Holy Spirit, who opened my eyes and heart to Scripture, where my Savior taught me and became my Freedom Minister. If He delivered me, He will deliver you, too. He did a great work in my family, too. The story of the woman with the anger issues in the chapter, "The Dark Shadow of Anger," was my mom's story. My life with her was terribly painful. However, when I turned my life over to Jesus, He healed the hurts she had inflicted.

Then, He sent me back to her and taught me about unconditional love and how to have a relationship with wounded people.

I learned how to set healthy boundaries, and I learned how to love someone without having an agenda of being loved in return. Jesus taught me that. He loved me for over thirty years when I never acknowledged Him. He loved me when my behavior made me totally unlikeable. When I could love her unconditionally, she finally felt safe enough to let Him love her.

I watched her come to know Him. Because He gave me the great honor of having her as a mom, I KNOW deep inside that His love is not conditional and that no matter what, He will never leave us. He gave me a new Legacy through His work in our family. It is a legacy of love. There is no greater legacy to leave.

We overcome by the Blood of the Lamb and the words of our testimony.[77] He wants us to fellowship with His other children to be encouraged by their testimonies about Him. Seek a place where you connect with His church. Ask for mentors who are walking free. He sent an army of women to walk with me on my path and then used me to walk with others. Open your eyes to find the ones He has for you.

Are you ready to see what comes next? The Lord's table is filled with every good and perfect thing He has prepared for you.

John has a powerful new testimony and a stirring message to help you cast your vision into the next season of the freedom journey. This awareness will be a great encouragement for all His children.

---

[77] As described in Revelation 12:11

דְּרוֹר

Chapter Twelve

Crossing Over

I spent many years oblivious that my heavenly Father was actively involved in my life. I know it is hard to believe, and I can guess what you are thinking, *"Sure, John, prove it to me. Because it is difficult for me to imagine a good Father would allow what has happened to me."* I had those beliefs as well. I, too, have been through physical and emotional trauma. Then my eyes were opened, and I realized He was there all along. Your eyes will be opened, and there will be freedom and justice for you. It is coming!

Angel and I moved to the Dallas-Fort Worth metroplex after I retired from the US Army in November 2018. We accepted a position with Dave Roever Ministries and spent four wonderful years learning from Dave and his team. On December 31, 2022, we transitioned out of Roever Ministries into what we thought was the unknown. It was scary and full of risk. I made a graphic design because of our situation that says, "Faith looks like RISK." We had a lot of concerns and questions regarding finances, what is next, do we start our own ministry or team up with someone? The list can go on forever, I am sure you understand.

I knew I had to get alone with God to hear Him clearly. I anticipated job offers but knew I was not to accept just anything. I knew God had something very specific coming. It did not take long before we received our first of multiple offers. Something inside me kept saying, *"No, wait."*

One morning while in prayer, I asked, *"Should I accept this offer? It seems perfect for us right now. We can use the money."* I heard that still, small voice in my heart, *"Wait."* One of our prayer team members called me that afternoon. He said, *"What do you need prayer for?"* I said, *"I am good. I do not have a prayer request."* He said, *"Okay, because I was praying for you, and I heard God say, 'Tell John wait upon the Lord."* Needless to say, my Father had my full attention, and I respectfully declined the offers. God was with us in our transition. It was hard to see Him because we were in panic mode, so He used those we trusted to confirm His presence. What a good Father!

I received another revelation around the same time. It warned me not to lean on my understanding and not to proceed without God's leading. You must understand this because God wants us to know He fully understands our situations. Flashy or familiar opportunities will be offered, but they will not be from God. Scary, right? We have to be like Moses and take this stand, *"God, if you are not the One moving me, then I am not going anywhere or accepting anything."*[78]

Here is a bit more context for the revelation. In the verses we shared about David being anointed as king, remember, God instructs the Prophet Samuel to go to Bethlehem, to the house of Jesse, for God had provided Himself a new king from among his sons. *"Furthermore,*

[78] Paraphrase of Exodus 33:15

God said, "...I will show you what you shall do; you shall anoint for Me **the one I name to you**."[79] In short, God was saying, "Do not try and figure out what you should do. I am with you and will direct you."

Samuel learned to hear God's voice at a young age and was experienced with executing His will. He was not the new guy; he was the veteran. He makes it to his destination and gets Jesse and his sons together. Then Samuel did what 99% of us would do; he leaned on his own understanding even after God told him, *"...you shall anoint...the one I name to you."* Samuel looks at Jesse's son Eliab and says, *"Surely, the Lord's anointed is before Him!"* Had God told Samuel, *"Eliab, that is My anointed?"* No.

Here is my interpretation of the situation. Samuel saw Eliab and said, "This is a no-brainer. This guy fits the mold. His physical features are similar to King Saul; surely this is the guy." Jesse had seven sons pass before Samuel, and still God had not named His future king. In fact, the future king was not even among the group. He was with the sheep. God showed me through this, *"Do not lean on your own understanding. Do not accept a position because it looks familiar, or it's from a large ministry, or because it looks flashy. I am with you and will guide you. Wait for Me!"* Don't settle for a good thing; wait for the God thing!

Around the same time, the church we attend was hosting their annual New Beginnings Conference. One of the staff members encouraged me to attend. I wasn't interested. I didn't want to be

---

[79] 1 Samuel 16:3, NKJV

around people. I wanted to be alone with God. I was grieving our departure from Roever Ministries, even though it was the right decision. I reluctantly attended the conference. I told myself, "I will go, but I am sitting in the back, away from everyone, because I need to hear from God." Oh, how foolish I was because my Father was the One orchestrating my attendance.

On night one, I arrived expecting to sit in the back of the auditorium. While standing in line waiting to check in, Pastor Troy Brewer, the conference host, saw me and headed directly to me. *"Hey, what are you up to?"* We chatted for a second then he said, *"Go to the Green Room. You are one of the VIPs."* Wait, I was supposed to hide from the world and grieve. Well, that was my plan, but my Father used Pastor Troy Brewer to pull me out of the pit I was putting myself into. I went to the conference expecting to hide out. What happened after I entered the building resembles a parable Jesus used to make an important point.

"So Jesus told a parable to those who were invited, when He noted how they chose the best places, saying to them: "When you are invited by anyone to a wedding feast, do not sit down in the best place, lest one more honorable than you be invited by him; and he who invited you and him come and say to you, 'Give place to this man,' and then you begin with shame to take the lowest place. But when you are invited, go and sit down in the lowest place, so that when he who invited you comes he may say to you, 'Friend, go up higher.' Then you will have glory in the presence of those who sit at the table with you. For whoever exalts himself will be humbled, and he who

humbles himself will be exalted."[80]

God used Pastor Troy to call me up higher. The conference started, and the VIPs were being introduced; then, Pastor Troy affirmed me before everyone in attendance. At that moment, I knew this was only possible because of God. There could not be another way. I was not even supposed to be there, and suddenly, I was being introduced from the stage.

Please hear my heart. The situation did not incite pride within me. No. Quite the opposite. It humbled me because I knew my heavenly Father had His eyes on me and my situation. By the end of night one, I had more conversations than I could count and prayed with numerous old and new friends. I was able to meet and talk with the other VIPs and got to know them behind the scenes.

There was one that stood out to me, Pastor Brian Bolt. While reading his bio I was stunned when it said he pastors a church in Whittier, CA. What?! I grew up in Whittier, CA, and I had yet to meet a pastor from my hometown. I was excited to meet him. I told Angel, *"There's a pastor from my hometown. I have to meet him."* She said, *"Maybe he'll invite you to speak at his church."* I thought, *"That would be epic, but he doesn't know me. Pastors don't let people they don't know preach at their church."* I said, *"I am not worried about that right now, even though it would be amazing to go home and preach."*

I met Pastor Brian on day two. I just about tackled him like a

---

[80] Luke 14:7-11, NKJV

groupie. I wanted him to know I was from Whittier and for him to hear our testimony. He was extremely courteous and even shared his personal cell number with me. Yet I didn't feel an immediate connection with him. Looking back on the situation, I realized he meets thousands of people. Not only is he a church pastor, but he speaks around the world. He doesn't jump up and down whenever he meets someone new; that is what I hoped would happen.

Fast forward to February 2023. Angel and I began planning a two-week visit to California. Two weeks on vacation was unusual for us because we were always working. We knew that we needed more time with our children and grandchildren. They wanted us to be around more, and we wanted the same thing. The Message Bible says, *"A good life gets passed on to the grandchildren; ill-gotten wealth ends up with good people."*[81] If you read other translations, you will conclude that the author is talking about wealth. For me, I take this scripture to mean legacy. Angel and I hope to leave God a legacy of worshippers from our family. It's not that I expect my children and grandchildren to follow my career path, though, because it is a calling. All I want is for them to love and worship the Lord with their whole heart. For that to happen, we need to be active in their lives.

During our planning, we decided to drive since we needed to take our dogs. We also wanted to tour the Grand Canyon while en route to California. I reached out to Pastor Brian, hoping he might know someone who had a rental home. He didn't know of anyone but

---

[81] Proverbs 13:22, MSG

replied with a question, *"Are you interested in speaking at my church on Wednesday, 29 March 2023?"* It took me 5 seconds to pray, ask God, and reply, *YES!*

When the conversation ended, I shouted in my home, *"Yes, yes, yes!"* I ran looking for Angel. "Babe, guess what?" Of course, I didn't wait for her to guess. I shouted, *"Do you remember we met Pastor Brian Bolt from Whittier?"* I eagerly said, *"He invited us to speak at his church."* We hugged and praised the Lord. Then I thought, *"Let me look up his church."* I ran to my computer and typed in his church's name. When it came up on my screen, I gasped, and my heart nearly stopped. I thought to myself, *"No way! This cannot be real. There is no way he pastors that church."*

When I was approximately five years old, there used to be a church bus that picked up families in our community. One Sunday morning, I was up before everyone else, watching cartoons. As usual, the bus pulled up, blaring its horn. I got up, and without changing my clothes or informing anyone, I got on the bus headed for church. When I arrived, the staff must have sensed I was alone because I was still in my pajamas. Somehow, they found out who I was and called my mom. She rushed and picked me up.

As I reflect on that moment, there was something that happened that marked my life forever. Because I went blindly as an innocent boy searching for God, I found Him. He marked me that day, saying, *"Today, I have become your Father."* The Bible says that when you search for God with your whole heart, He will be found.[82] While I searched the internet for Pastor Brian's church, the results flashed on my monitor. It was the same church where 40 years earlier, I first met my Heavenly Father. At the moment of that realization, I began to cry because what are the odds something like this could happen? For most of those forty years, I didn't walk with God. But He was walking with me. Unfortunately, as He walked with me, God had to witness some terrible things while I lived in my own Lo-Debar. Regardless of my choices, He passionately pursued me until I surrendered.

In my Spirit, I knew March 29th, 2023, was a significant day, and I was returning to that church for a reason. I couldn't figure it out, though. I asked God, *"What is the significance of that day?"* No reply. *Oh well,* I thought, *it must not be important.*

The day came for me to speak. I was excited about the opportunity, and several family members were coming to the service. My son, John, was taking his family, and it would be my grandson's first church service. The Lord is a redemptive Father; just read through the Prodigal Son parable in Luke 15.

The redemption story being played out before me was that I grew up without my dad, which caused me to live as an orphan. I ran after the world's goods and away from God. Forty years after I first met my true Father, He led me full circle to the place I first met Him. He went even further when He invited my legacy to the same church.

---

[82] From Jeremiah 29:11-13

He was showing me He wanted to do the same with them, and, on this day, He was using me as their preacher!

Several weeks after we returned from our visit, I read an article by a minister talking about the book of Joshua. He shared numerous scriptures from the first five chapters with commentary, then he concluded by saying we are Crossing Over. Everything he wrote lit a fire inside me. God was speaking to me. I began to meditate on the Scriptures he shared, and suddenly it hit me. We are Crossing Over into our promise after 40 years in the wilderness.

Let me explain. God tells Joshua, *"Moses My servant is dead. Now therefore, __arise__, go over this Jordan, you and all this people, to the land which I am giving to them—the children of Israel."*[83] **"Three days later,** the Israelite officers went through the camp, giving these instructions to the people: *"When you see the Levitical priests carrying the Ark of the Covenant of the Lord your God, move out from your positions and follow them. Since you have never traveled this way before, they will guide you."*[84] *"The people crossed the Jordan on __the tenth day of the first month.__"*[85]

The revelation was exploding inside me. Here's how I saw it, *"Joshua, get up! In three days, you will cross over the Jordan River with the people going from the desert to the promised land."* But something was missing. I wasn't seeing everything; then it hit me. Look up the actual day they crossed over, which was the Hebrew

---

83 Joshua 1:2, NKJV
[83] Joshua 1:2, NKJV
[84] Joshua 3:2-4, NKJV
[85] Joshua 4:19, NKJV

month of Nissan on the 10th day.

I rushed to get my copy of Pastor Troy Brewer's calendar, *"Looking Up."* In it, he includes the Hebrew and Gregorian months and days. I quickly flipped through it to the month of Nissan. Okay, now the tenth day. I gasped! If Joshua had **crossed over** with the people in 2023, it would have been Saturday, April 1st, 2023. However, the day God told Joshua to **arise** (Get Up) would have been Wednesday, March 29th, 2023, the day I returned after 40 years to the church where I first met my Father.

I walked into that church at 5 years old, and my heavenly Father put a call on my life that day. From that point, there was a spiritual war to destroy my life which included losing my dad, gangs, drugs, war, and being shot point blank in the throat with a .45 caliber. My entire life was similar to Mephibosheth's.

I was royalty, but I lived in the wilderness (Lo-debar) until I was invited to go higher and returned to the King's table and to my true identity that I am a son of God. I ran around like an orphan my entire life, but I just now realized that my Father was running with me the whole time.

Joshua leads the Israelites from the wilderness, where they had been for **40 years,** to the promised land. Then God leads me back to the church where I first met Him **40 years** later. When God spoke to Joshua regarding crossing over, He said, "**Arise**." Remember, according to the calendars, that day would have been 29 March, the day I returned to the church. On 2 April 2014, as my blood poured from my neck after being shot at Fort Hood military base, God spoke to me audibly as he spoke to Joshua, "John, **<u>Get Up</u>**!"

God sent me back to that church in Whittier on a date that memorialized the moment, thousands of years before, when God spoke to His children to lead them into the promised land. He told Joshua to "Arise." To me, He said, "Get Up." There are too many coincidences not to see God's intervention. **We are Crossing Over!**

I pray that through this, your eyes have been opened. YOU HAVE NEVER BEEN AN ORPHAN. You have a Father, and he has always loved you. It is time you return to your rightful place in the palace, which is the Kings table.

Get Up!

Hear the words you have longed to hear from your Father,

"You are My Beloved Son;
in You, I am well pleased."

Take Possession

God came to the Israelites who were sitting just outside the land He promised to give them and said,

> *"You have stayed at this mountain long enough.*
> *It is time to break camp and move on.*
> *Look, I am giving all this land to you!*
> *Go in and possess it."*[86]

It was the plan He had for His children and for all their descendants. He brought them to a place where they would live freely and prosper. He wants to bring us into a place like that so we can know Him intimately and let Him guide us into every good thing He has for us.

When it was time for them to cross over, Joshua was leading the people through the instructions God gave Him and said,

"Attention! Listen to what God, your God, has to say. This is how you'll know that God is alive among you—he will completely dispossess before you the Canaanites, Hittites, Hivites, Perizzites, Girgashites, Amorites, and Jebusites.

Look at what's before you: the Chest of the Covenant. Think of it—the Master of the entire earth is crossing the Jordan as you watch. Now take twelve men from the tribes of Israel, one man from each tribe. When the soles of the feet of the priests carrying the Chest of God, Master of all the earth, touch the Jordan's water, the flow of water will be stopped—the water coming from upstream will pile up

---

[86] Deut. 1:6-8 NLT

in a heap.[87]

God fulfilled every promise He made to His people and put this in the Scriptures to give us instruction today. If you are at your place of crossing over, let Holy Spirit reveal the elements in this Scriptural account that relate to your life.

Have you been "camped out" in repeating destructive patterns in your life? Many of us came from families that had these patterns for generations. If this fits you, do you hear what God, *your God*, said? You've stayed there too long. Break camp! Ask Holy Spirit to reveal the beliefs you have hammered into your life to hold it all in place. Then ask for His help to pull them up.

Visualize the priests carrying the Ark of the Covenant. They had the presence of God with them. When they came to the Jordan, they had to stop walking the way they were and touch their foot to the water.

Jesus is the High Priest for all eternity, and He lives in you, so He is coming with you. What is your obstacle? What troubled waters will you have to walk through to cross over? Whatever it is, you will have to take that big step of faith. It is a big step, but He is with you. You may feel frightened. That's okay to feel the fear; but take the step of faith. God told Joshua three different times to be "strong and courageous" because He knows how scary it can feel.

God will displace the source of your chaos and confusion when you cross over and close the door to the enemy. He is telling

---

[87] Quotes and paraphrases from Deu. 1:7-8, NLT

you to "possess" what He has given you. Take back everything that has been taken from you. He will restore your relationships. Particularly with your dad or mom. Even if they are no longer in your life, He can change your perception and understanding of them and change that ache inside you. He can restore your innocence and your childhood. He would love to hear you laugh again and experience pure JOY over simply living the life He has for you. He can't change your past, but He can and will change your future and give you back your *hope* for yourself and for your family.

It's been long enough. Take a step of faith and prayerfully walk with Holy Spirit guiding you through the freedom exercises that you are going to find in these last pages.

God's perfect plan is to provide a way for us to be saved from the life we have been living and come live with Him in His kingdom of Heaven on earth. He had it written down in the Scriptures so it is easy to understand. You may have heard it referred to as the Roman Road, and it has helped thousands understand God's plan. Prayerfully read through God's Words, asking for His Help to follow His Ways.

THE ROMAN ROAD

OUR PROBLEM
Romans 3:23
For everyone has sinned; we all fall short of God's glorious standard.

Romans 3:10-18
As the Scriptures say, No one is righteous, not even one. No one is truly wise; no one is seeking God. All have turned away; all have become useless. No one does good, not a single one. Their talk is foul, like the stench from an open grave. Their tongues are filled with lies. Snake venom drips from their lips. Their mouths are full of cursing and bitterness. They rush to commit murder. Destruction and misery always follow them. They don't know where to find peace. They have no fear of God at all.

Romans 6:23
For the wages of sin is death, but the free gift of God is eternal life through Christ Jesus our Lord.

OUR HOPE
Romans 5:8
But God showed his great love for us by sending Christ to die for us while we were still sinners.

OUR RESPONSE
Romans 10:9
If you openly declare that Jesus is Lord and believe in your heart that God raised him from the dead, you will be saved.

Romans 10:13
Everyone who calls on the name of the Lord will be saved.

OUR SALVATION
Romans 5:1
Therefore, since we have been made right in God's sight by faith, we have peace with God because of what Jesus Christ our Lord has done for us.

Romans 8:1
So now there is no condemnation for those who belong to Christ Jesus.

OUR ASSURANCE
Romans 8:38-39
And I am convinced that nothing can ever separate us from God's love. Neither death nor life, neither angels nor demons, neither our fears for today nor our worries about tomorrow—not even the powers of hell can separate us from God's love. No power in the sky above or in the earth below— indeed, nothing in all creation will ever be able to separate us from the love of God that is revealed in Christ Jesus our Lord.

SALVATION PRAYER

If you have been prompted by this text to accept Jesus as your personal, powerful Savior, or, to re-establish your relationship with Him, this prayer will help you invite Him into your heart and your life.

Dear Lord Jesus,

I need You. I know that I am a sinner, and I ask for Your forgiveness. I believe You died for my sins and that You rose from the dead. Thank You for forgiving my sins and giving me eternal life. I turn from my sins and invite You to come into my heart and life and lead me. I want to trust and follow You as my Lord and Savior. Help me be who You created me to be. Amen.

If you pray this prayer from a sincere heart, reach out to a parent, pastor, minister, or another believer to let us know you are now part of our family.

Breaking of Strongholds

When Jesus stood up in the Temple, picked up the Scroll of Isaiah, and began to read, He announced His ministry. He named many ways He would accomplish His mission through many avenues, but His summation sentence ties them all together. He said He came *"To set at liberty those who are oppressed."* The mission of His ministry is to free the oppressed![88] He is a freedom-focused Savior who ministers Freedom to those who come to Him.

Because we live in a broken world, our souls are impacted by many things that happen in our childhood. If you are a wounded child of a wounded child, you may have set up strongholds in your soul that created a repeating negative pattern of behavior. By definition, a stronghold is a place that has been fortified to protect it against attack.

You set up ways to avoid more pain and to keep yourself from being vulnerable to attacks. Depending on your circumstances, your strongholds may have been established to ensure your survival.

Process of Forming Strongholds

Trauma or Negative
Event

Responses to
Our Defensive Efforts

Conclusion Drawn
Lie is Formed

Avoid Further Pain
Set Up Defense Plan

---

[88] Luke 4:18, NKJV

Looking at people's lives will help us look into our own souls. One example of how this gets set up is the story of Robby. He was the son of a successful business owner who was a "self-made" man. His dad was consumed by his work and demanded a lot from himself to run a tight ship and turn a good profit. There was little time for family and little attention from him when he was with his family. Robby was given responsibilities for household chores and lawn care. He was always expected to make good grades. Schoolwork was never a problem until Robby got to junior high. His math class was taught by a first-year teacher who wasn't very patient or very good at giving examples or explaining. Robby had a low math grade when the first report card came home. That sent his dad into a rage that got out of control. He unleashed a barrage of demeaning labels at Robby, ultimately delivering a hard slap to his son. The trauma culminated in a threat that had believability in Robby's heart, *"You better get that grade up and never let this happen again, or you will be sorry."* The following report card came home with an A in math. Robby was very excited to share this incredible, hard-won success with his dad. However, after a quick glance at the grades, all his dad said was, *"You should have always had that. See that it stays there!"*

The stronghold began with this dad running his family like a business. Robby was never nurtured or told how much he was loved, nor was he ever simply enjoyed. He concluded that his only value was in how he performed. He began to demand a great deal from himself to avoid further pain. His performance prevented his dad's negative responses, reinforcing his conclusion and strengthening his behavior. Since his efforts to overcome the challenging class were demeaned, he understood that he didn't matter; all that mattered was performance.

Let's also consider a friend named Nicole. She was a long-awaited child and the first grandchild on both sides of the family. From the day she was born, the family said she looked "just like her dad, Nick." Throughout her development, she heard, "She walks just like him; she sounds just like her dad; she is so good at baseball, just like Nick was." Now, you may be thinking; This *sounds very loving and supportive.* That's how we sometimes get off base. This girl followed after her dad, trying to do what he did and be like him. He was a pastor. She went to Bible college and followed him into the ministry. She always pushed herself to be perfect; after all, she had always been told how important it was to her dad for her to be "good."

Then the unimaginable happened. Her dad had a great big, highly visible, very public moral failure. He destroyed his marriage, friendships, and standings with the church and decimated this girl's heart. She heard what others were saying about him now. She went slinking away from all religious affiliations. She withdrew from life and wanted only to live in obscurity. Over the next few years, she underwent three hospital stays with intense treatments for bulimia and anorexia.

Her stronghold had been put in place shortly after her birth. The adverse event was that she was denied her right to become who she was sent to Earth to become. The lie she came to believe was that she was the same person as her dad. Her only defense was to mimic him so she could be like him. The negative response was that people affirmed that she was just like her dad. That strengthened the stronghold, and the destructive behavior continued. This was interrupted by her dad's moral failure and all the judgments about him that people around her made about who her dad really was.

Since her only identity was as a replica of her dad, she internalized those demeaning pronouncements people had made, saw herself as evil and hedonistic, and believed the antichrist also controlled her. She stopped feeding herself as punishment. She withdrew from people because one of her lies-turned-to-truths was that she would hurt people too much, so she didn't want to be around them. She never wanted to marry because she believed she should never have children since they might be like her.

Both of these people finally ran into the depth of darkness, where repeating patterns always take us. They both cried out to God, who spoke a rhema word to them. Both of them let Him lead their lives and were able to break the strongholds and live their lives as God intended.

He gave us His words to assure us and to guide us:

"Be sure of this: I am with you always, even to the end of the age. The thief's purpose is to steal and kill and destroy. I came to give you a rich and satisfying life.

Moses put a veil over his face so the people of Israel would not see the glory, even though it was destined to fade away. But the people's minds were hardened, and to this day whenever the old covenant is being read, the same veil covers their minds so they cannot understand the truth. And this veil can be removed only by believing in Christ.

But whenever someone turns to the Lord, the veil is taken away. For the Lord is the Spirit, and wherever the Spirit of the Lord is, there is freedom. So all of us who have had that veil removed can see and reflect the glory of the Lord. And the Lord—who is the Spirit—makes us more and more like him as we are changed into his glorious image.

But remember, you are human, but you don't wage war as humans do. You use God's mighty weapons, not worldly weapons, to knock down the **strongholds** of your **human reasoning** and to destroy **false arguments**. You can destroy every **proud obstacle** that keeps you from knowing God. Let me show you how to capture your rebellious thoughts so they obey My teachings.

My Kingdom is here, it is right at your hand, reach out and lay claim to your place in My Kingdom.

I want to give you the fullness of My Holy Spirit to guide you; remember, all you have to do is ask for more, and it will be given to you."[89]

---

[89] Paraphrased from John 10:10, Matthew 28:20, 2 Corinthians 3:13-18, 1 Corinthians 10:3-5, Luke 11:13

Knocking Down Strongholds

This is a time of prayerful connection with Holy Spirit. Commit to a time and establish a place where you seek Him. It is helpful to have a notebook; you will need to make notes about things that come up. As you pray, you are having a dialogue with God through the Holy Spirit. You can keep your eyes open and write as you dialogue with Him. You will want to write down His rhema words. You will identify lies; He will give you the Truth to break those out of your mind. He may prompt you to write out more; be ready.

Your freedom requires radical honesty. This is not a place for glossing over or making excuses. You can't change your past, but understanding through the help of Holy Spirit will provide the power for you to have a redeemed future. These processes are "frameworks" for your time with Him. It guides you, but be open to Holy Spirit to prompt different questions or ideas.

Identify the repeating patterns in your life.

What has shown up repeatedly in different ways in different relationships and situations, but you know it is a persistent problem in your life? He is, and always has been, with you. He knows. He wants you to talk to Him about it.

What are the past hurts or trauma?

What difficult things did you experience? What should you have experienced that you didn't? What is in your life that came through your family, your culture, or through your physical genetics? What shouldn't have happened that did~

> Abuse
> Abandonment
> Neglect
> Sin; with no forgiveness, leaving shame, guilt, remorse

What should have happened that didn't~

> Nurture
> Provision
> Respect, Honor
> Forgiveness
> Love – freely given
> Sense of Self-Worth and Identity

What hurts keep happening in different situations?

Identify the Lies

Be sure to take enough time on the following questions and write down *anything* that stirs your heart. As you work through this, leave room to ask other questions that come to mind. These are offered to provoke your thoughts.

What do you believe about the following?

1.   <u>Yourself</u> –

What do you say internally about yourself?

When you look in the mirror, do you look yourself in the eyes?

What do you say to the person in the mirror?

What are your thoughts about yourself when you go through a repeating pattern?

2.   Other People -

What do you say about specific people in your life? What do you believe about significant people like parents, siblings, and close associates? What about groups of people; like "men," "women," "teachers," "preachers," and "bosses"? What about classifications of people, like race, ethnicity, or denomination?

3.   God –

How do you see Father God? Describe Him in detail. How close to Him do you see yourself standing when you visualize Him?

Who is Jesus? Imagine walking down a road and suddenly meeting Him face to face. What do you think that would be like?

When you think of Holy Spirit being in you, what do you think?

Describe how you feel when you know you hear God.

How do you think God see you?

Take Down Defenses

Trauma in our lives creates a desire to be sure we have a good defense in place so that we never have to go through that pain again. Anger is often used to keep other people at a distance so they won't hurt us. There are many strategies for survival put in place by hurt people. High performance, over-achieving, numbing, withdrawal, becoming a class or family clown, and rebellion against all forms of authority are some of the many ways people try to defend themselves. Freedom requires us to take down the defenses we have put into place and seek the only One Who can truly defend us. Be courageous enough to identify your defenses and be willing to let them go.

The Process

God wants you Saved, Healed, and Set Free. Then He will lead you to be Discipled and Equipped. When you are, He will Empower you to Serve in His Kingdom.

God could have spoken "Universe," and it would have been created in a Holy Second. He took six days, though, because He wants us to know He is a God of Process. Your life is a process, and He will guide you and show you more of His Character and Nature every step of the way. Press in; the work is well worth your efforts and time.

1. Ask Holy Spirit to show you **the first time** you felt the pain associated with your repeating pattern. Don't discount anything you see or remember. It is important.

2. Ask Jesus to show you where He was during that situation. He wants to show you where He was, and He has important Truth to talk to you about.

3. Open up to a dialogue about the entire situation. Remember Holy Spirit is in you to comfort you, keep you safe, and guide you into all Truth.

4. Ask for help to identify what conclusions you drew and what beliefs you formed there in that first situation. What meaning did you assign to this event? Which of your beliefs about this are handed down from others?

5. Ask Jesus if those lies and things you believed are true? Listen carefully. If they aren't true, ask Him what the truth is. He wants to speak into this; listen to Him.

6. Confess the lies you have believed; tell Him what false beliefs you have about yourself, other people, and God.

7. Repent by acknowledging you are releasing those all from your life.

8. Ask, from a genuine desire in your heart, if Jesus will forgive you for believing those wrong things. Listen until you hear His answer.

9. When He forgives you, truly accept that grace, mercy, and forgiveness into your soul.

10. Forgive yourself. Highly value what He did on the cross be accepting His forgiveness.

11. Ask Jesus to show you anyone you need to forgive. If He prompts something, write it down.

12. Say the Truth that He has spoken to you aloud. Confess that you believe it with your whole heart. Write it down. Ask for Holy Spirit to show you the Scriptures where this is recorded. Memorize them!

13. Ask Jesus to show you the defenses you have used so you can protect yourself.

14. Get clear on the ways you learned to protect yourself from pain or to seek comfort.

15. Confess and receive forgiveness for what you have done because of these defenses.

16. Ask Him to show you the people you have hurt through your defenses. Ask Holy Spirit to guide you to know how to go to those people, confess, make amends, and ask them if they will forgive you.

17. Renounce your defense. Invite the Lord to be your defender. Lord, would You show me a picture of what it would be like for You to protect me? How do You want to comfort me?

18. Believe He will do this and say this Truth aloud.

Your Soul is where your will lives. As you do this work, you must ask for Holy Spirit **to strengthen you** and **align your will with God's will** for your life. Tune your ears to listen to and obey Spirit's prompting. Remember, these promptings probably will not seem "normal." You may get prompted to change some things that you will resist, such as playlists, playmates, and playgrounds. He will put a new song in your heart and lead you to better people, places, and things if you align your will with His.

Forgiveness

Forgiveness is God's provision for releasing us from the power and pain of sins committed against us. Through it, we receive the healing benefit of Jesus' work on the cross. The devil's strategy is to keep us from healing and from being loving.

If you haven't released the pain, you aren't released from the power it has over you.

Jesus died for the sins you committed. He also died for the sins committed against you.

If you are a wounded child of a wounded child, forgiveness will be a huge part of your healing. If the silence from your absent parent's unspoken words of affirmation still echoes in your soul, then it may be time to let Holy Spirit speak to you. Ask for revelations about your parent.

The stories of Robby and Nicole were told at the beginning of these exercises. They each went through a healing journey that helped them claim the freedom that was there for them. They both discovered their dads had their own struggles, leading to pain in their families. That discovery helped each of them stop blaming their dad and feel compassion in their heart for him. Once that happened, they had a new perspective on their own journey. Once they forgave their dad and removed the bitterness, they began to see the positive character traits they had gained through what they had been through.

Robby was ultimately able to work with his dad and step into leadership in the family business. He valued his hard work ethic and the value he placed on excellence. However, his leadership differed from his dad's since he lived by a Scripture Jesus gave him during his forgiveness process. His benchmark is, *"Work willingly at whatever you do, as though you were working for the Lord rather than for people."*[90]

Once Jesus healed his heart, he could hear the Lord tell him, *"My love and my presence are here with you, no matter what."* Robby knew it was the Lord because that was so different from what he had been told throughout his life. His soul believed it because it had been longing to hear that forever!

Nicole's dad's choices left deep soul wounds and required a long journey. She had run as far away from her dad as possible, intending never to see him again. Holy Spirit never left her, even though she refused to open up and talk to the Lord about the pain. She journeyed as far into the darkness as she could live through. She even began to want death as a way to end the pain. As she decided and turned toward total darkness, an unbidden question came out of her soul, *"God, if you are real, will you show yourself to me? Who are you? Are you here?"*

In a blinding light encounter, she heard his voice. He said, *"Sweet Precious One, I am here; I have never left you. I love who you are too much to ever leave your side. This is how I see you."* Nicole was stunned when she heard His words and saw the vision He gave her. He took her back to a time when she was around ten years old

---

[90] Col. 3:23, NLT

and was taken shopping by her aunt. She talked her aunt into letting her get a pink, frilly, girly dress she loved. Later, when she showed it to her dad, he told her she needed to return it. *"It just doesn't look like something you should wear,"* he said. Her clothes were tailored; many were blue, her dad's favorite color.

She believed God's rhema word that day. He called her "precious," and she had always been called "buddy," "little pal," or "slugger." She knew the vision came from Him. It was the vision she had of her true self which she had been made to deny. She forgave her dad as God showed her more about his life, too. She later said forgiving him had truly been the piece that helped her become what God wanted her to be. She is a counselor who specializes in recovery from eating disorders. She explained that if she had held on to the bitterness, it would have poisoned her input into other women's lives. That was a journey she wasn't willing to take.

Forgiveness takes courage and the desire to be truly free. If you are ready, the process is laid out for you next. It begins when we become willing to step off the judge's bench in the courtroom of our hearts and let God sit there.

The Lord wants to relieve you from the weight of all the sins you have borne.

The 2-Step Process:

Choose to forgive

Allows you to regain control of your mind
Empowers you
Frees you from the label of Victim
Connects you Ever Closer to Him
Acknowledges What He Did For You

Entrust the consequences of the sin to the Father

Unhealed hurt festers within you like a splinter in the heart.
He can't heal your hurt and pain unless you submit it to Him.
Let Him heal the hurt, He then gives you a different view of the situation

Points from the chapter on Forgiveness to remember:

- If someone in your life hurts you, Jesus teaches us to go and talk with them about it. That often paves the way to reconciling the relationship and bringing everyone involved closer to the Lord.

- If that is not possible or safe, forgiveness will happen as you transfer them out of your heart and ask the Lord to be over them. He is a Just God. He knows the situation, and He will honor you. You matter to Him, and He will bring justice.

- Wounded people wound people. If you are holding unforgiveness against someone from your past, remember they may have been wounded and unhealed. God does not want you to be a bitter, wounded person who continues to hurt others because of your unhealed pain. Jesus paid a great price for your forgiveness. He gave it to you freely. He wants to set you free so you can offer forgiveness to others on your path.

Forgiveness Process

The healing that results from forgiveness can be immediate. Many times, it opens the door to the process of healing.

1. Seek the Lord and bring this person and situation with you. Talk with Him, ask questions you need Him to answer. Ask to see all of this situation the way He does. Radical honesty is required. Tell Jesus what they did and the feelings you had because of it. Ask Jesus to speak to you about the other person. Ask Him to help you see them the way He does. Listen to Him and keep asking for His help with this.

2. Tell Him about the bitterness in your heart. Tell Him how you believed that you don't matter. Tell Him how unfair you think it was. Tell Him you don't believe the other person deserves to be forgiven. Tell the Lord everything.

3. Identify the lies and beliefs you formed from this situation. Ask Holy Spirit to guide you into all Truth.

4. Ask to see the other person the way Jesus does. Ask for a Supernatural understanding of the entire situation.

5. Ask Jesus to help you release the pain. Ask Him to please take the bitterness in your emotions and the lasting effects out of your life.

6. Ask Him to help you release the other person. You can't change the past, but you are standing at a place where you can decide if you are willing to allow Jesus to change your future and the future of those coming behind you in your family.

Heart-Prayer for Meditation as you prepare yourself to forgive.

Lord, I am willing to forgive and let go of everything in my past. I give this person to you and trust you to heal my heart. I willingly give grace and mercy instead of blame and condemnation. As an act of my will, I choose to forgive all those who have hurt me, harmed me, or spoken against me. I free them in my thoughts and no longer hold their sins against them. I ask You to bless them in Your mercy. I do this by Your indwelling power.

Thank You that I am a brand-new creation! All the old has passed away, and I stand clean in Your sight. I choose to receive your healing grace by the cleansing power of the Holy Spirit within me. Jesus, thank you for taking all sin and its bitterness to the cross so that I can now be free from the pain and from the power it had in my life. I receive all Your blessings for my life and give You all praise, honor, and glory. Amen!

Freedom From Fear

There are Rational Fears that are God-given natural responses when our physical or psychological safety is threatened. These keep us safe and alert to dangers; they are sensible and give us caution.

Fear is part of God's Holy Design. It is the beginning of wisdom. *The fear of the Lord is the beginning of knowledge, but fools despise wisdom and instruction.*[91]

Irrational Fears, however, are without reason or understanding and cause stress in our lives. This is where the enemy seeks to establish strongholds. These can be at the root of spiritual bondage. Behind every irrational fear is a lie.

Fear is the first emotion mentioned in the Bible. Adam said, *"I heard Your voice in the garden, and I was afraid because I was naked, and I hid myself."*[92] If we are afraid to do something, it may be that the enemy has given us a spirit of fear of failing God. We must ask Holy Spirit to reveal any deep, unhealed wounds from our past which left us feeling terrified. They will operate in our life to take away our confidence in ourselves and our abilities.

This well-known Scripture gives us insight into how to break free from the bondage of fear. *"For God has not given us a spirit of fear, but of power and of love and of a sound mind."* The demon spirit of fear is sent to stop the work God has called us to do. This verse shows us God's gift to us to is have power, love, and a sound mind.

---

[91] Proverbs 1:7, NKJV
[92] In Genesis 3:10, NKJV

Most Prevalent Fears:

Fear of Death
This fear often has other fears that are rooted in it.

Its focus centers on 4 main issues:
- Fear of dying and going to hell; has its roots in being afraid we committed the unpardonable sin
- Fear of dying and leaving loved ones behind
- Fear of loved ones dying
- Fear of the dying process – the possible pain involved in dying

Paul addressed this fear in many places. He came very close to dying many times, so the Lord had shown him great truth in this area. *We are confident, yes, well pleased rather to be absent from the body and to be present with the Lord.*[93]

Fear of Rejection
If we fear being rejected, we are focused on acceptance or popularity instead of seeking God so we can know His love. God is love, and He created us to love. Love is our greatest need, and rejection is one of our greatest fears. Some of the deepest scars in our souls come from the times we felt rejected.

Fear of Failure
- If a person fears failure, they are looking for their identity in success. It is connected to the need for approval from others as well.

- If you are driven to have money, you fear poverty.

---

[93] 2 Corinthians 5:8, NKJV

- If you are driven to have power, you fear being overpowered or powerless, or insignificant.

- If you are driven to have position or influence, you have a fear of man, which is a craving for approval coupled with a fear of rejection.

- The root of control is fear. The lie is, "If I control my environment, I won't get hurt."

Symptoms of Fear

Apprehension	Heaviness	Superstitions
Anxiety	Horror	Tension
Burdens	Insomnia	Timidity
Extreme	Nervousness	Weariness
Caution	Nightmares	Worry
Fatigue	Phobias	Trembling
Fretting	Restlessness	Torment
Fright	Stress	Terror

The enemy uses lies that seem real to us to create strongholds of fear to keep us from God's plans and purposes for our lives.

No attribute of God is opposed more than His Perfect Love! It is the #1 target of the enemy's weapons.

These false beliefs MUST be exposed and replaced by the Truth of God's Word. The thoughts we don't take captive take us captive.

Possessing God's love results in fearless confidence in God and gives us the ability to love others. It is the love of God that casts out all fear!!

"There's no fear in love; but perfect love casts out fear because fear involves torment. He who fears has not been made perfect in love." [94]

---

[94] 1 John 4:18, NKJV

Fear = Lack of Faith

Jesus linked fear to a lack of faith. While Jesus was peacefully sleeping, a massive storm arose on the sea. The disciples came to Jesus, fearing for their lives. He said to His disciples, "Why are you fearful, O you of little faith?"[95]

We may have faith that God *can* do all things, but without a close intimate relationship with Him, we can't know how much He truly loves us. If we don't know that, we may struggle to believe that He *will* do those things for us.

The Opposite of Fear is not courage – It is LOVE! We must come to know God's love completely!! This is necessary for us to have complete faith in Him to overcome our fears. When we KNOW the Lord is with us, then we know He will work all things out for our good.

Freedom Process for Fear

1. Identify the fear and the root, or beginning of the fear and the lie that came out of that time.

2. Identify the need to protect yourself.

3. Confess your lack of faith in believing He CAN take care of you in all situations.

4. Confess your lack of faith that He WILL take care of you in all situations. Talk to Him about this and ask Him to show you why you lack faith in Him. Ask Him if He loves you enough to take care of you. Listen to His answer.

5. Renounce your fears.

---

[95] Matt. 8:26, NKJV

6. Repent by turning to Him and trusting Him; that will free you to love others.
7. Receive God's perfect love; confess that over yourself and life.
8. Submit to God and ask for a plan to face and overcome the fear. Ask Him to show you Scripture to build your faith and trust in Him; memorize them.

In one of his sermons, Charles Spurgeon said, *"I have a great need for Christ; I have a Great Christ for Every need."* That is so true and a great reminder that He cares about every detail of our lives. There are 365 verses of Scripture about fear, one for every day of the year because He knows how hard the world can seem to us at times. Here are a few to help us identify what may be at the root of our fears:

The fear of the LORD *is* the beginning of knowledge,
But fools despise wisdom and instruction. Proverbs 1:7

I sought the LORD, and He heard me,
And delivered me from all my fears. Psalm 34:4

There is no fear in love; but perfect love casts out fear, because fear involves torment. But he who fears has not been made perfect in love. 1 John 4:18

For God has not given us a spirit of fear,
but of power and of love and of a sound mind.
2 Timothy 1:7

Inasmuch then as the children have partaken of flesh and blood, He Himself likewise shared in the same, that through death He might destroy him who had the power of death, that is, the devil, and release those who through fear of death were all their lifetime subject to bondage. Hebrews 2:14-15

To grant us that we, being delivered from the hand of our enemies, might serve Him without fear, in holiness and righteousness before Him all the days of our life.
Luke 1:74-75

For you did not receive the spirit of bondage again to fear, but you received the Spirit of adoption by whom we cry out, "Abba, Father."
Romans 8:15

So we may boldly say: "The LORD *is* my helper; I will not fear. What can man do to me?"
Hebrews 13:6

Yea, though I walk through the valley of the shadow of death, I will fear no evil; For You *are* with me; Your rod and Your staff, they comfort me.
Psalm 23:4

The LORD *is* my light and my salvation; Whom shall I fear? The LORD *is* the strength of my life; Of whom shall I be afraid?
Psalm 27:1

The fear of man brings a snare, But whoever trusts in the Lord shall be safe.
Proverbs 29:25

Process for Overcoming Family Iniquity

Begin with a time of prayer as you seek God with all your heart. This is a framework for breaking the curses and entrenched iniquity in your family.

Thank you, Lord, for my father, mother, and the generations who have gone before me. Thank You for the good I've reaped because of their labors. Thank you, Lord, for my husband's father, mother, and generations before him. I confess that we come from a family that's less than perfect. I understand that our ancestors' sins and iniquities influence our spiritual heritage. I acknowledge this heritage to You today to receive Your promise of cleansing and restoration.

The sins and iniquities of these ancestors include (make a list)

I place these and any unknown sins our forefathers committed and all the consequences and effects of sin to the cross of Jesus Christ.

I place the blood of Jesus between myself and all generational sins on both the maternal and paternal sides of my family.

I ask that the blood of Jesus cleanse my family bloodlines all the way back to Adam.

I break all contracts, covenants, alliances, vows, hexes, or curses between me and my father, my mother, and all their ancestors and descendants. I break all contracts, covenants, alliances, vows, hexes, or curses between me, my in-laws, and all their ancestors and descendants.

Jesus, Your Word tells me you went to the cross to destroy the works of the devil. I ask You to come into my family and destroy and transform all patterns of sin committed through the works of the devil.

I renounce and break all demonic ancestral bondage.

In the Name of Jesus, in the Authority He has given me, and through His Power, I speak specifically to the spirit of fear, heaviness, stupor, deafness, dumbness, perversity, lying, error, infirmity, divination, whoredoms, bondage, anti-Christ, jealousy, and haughtiness. I tell you that you have no right, no power, or authority in my life. Bloodline curses are NOW broken. Therefore, I command all works of the enemy to leave now and go to the place Jesus has prepared for you.

I now set loose and receive all blessings that have come through my bloodlines upon me, my children, and future generations in Jesus' name.

I bind all familiar spirits and ask Jesus to send His angels to encamp around me and my family's descendants. Jesus, hide me under the shadow of Your wings. Thank You for delivering me from darkness unto light.

I declare that any curse that attempts to come upon me or my family line from this day forth must come through the cross of Jesus Christ and will be transformed from a curse to a blessing.

I confess that I have been made a new creation in Christ and have been given a new heritage. I claim my heritage in Christ and confess that in Him, I am Free.

Thank You for giving me, my children, and my future descendants a new heritage and a new future.

Thank You, Lord Jesus, for setting me free today.   *Amen*

Simplified Warfare

Seek the Lord, and follow this framework when you sense there is an open door to the enemy or that you feel a demonic attack.

In the Name and

in and through the Power and

of the Authority of Jesus Christ~

Cast Off any demons – command them to leave

Bind any demons and command them not to return.

Declare NO lasting effects on your life from this attachment.

Cancel the consequences of all that has happened.

Proclaim the Truth of God and **confess** that you now believe it.

Bind God's Truth to your heart.

Binding Truth to your heart is critical. Consider these verses,

"When an unclean spirit goes out of a man, he goes through dry places, seeking rest; and finding none, he says, 'I will return to my house from which I came.' And when he comes, he finds it swept and put in order. Then he goes and takes with him seven other spirits more wicked than himself, and they enter and dwell there, and the last state of that man is worse than the first."[96]

Filling our hearts with Truth prevents unclean spirits from returning to our lives.

---

[96] Matthew 12: 43-45, NKJV

Overview of Freedom Processes

The enemy of our soul is very diverse in his attacks and methods.

The process of freedom presented here is not a "cut-in-stone" process. You don't have a certain thing to do or a certain way to do it. The process is to enter the presence of Holy Spirit, talk to Jesus about all the shadows from your past, and listen to what He has to say to you.

Remember, Jesus has your freedom; He is the one who wanted your freedom so much that He came to Earth to provide it. He knows what is holding you hostage. He knows how to help you find your way to the life He has for you.

<u>An Overview of the Freedom Process:</u>

~Prayerfully invite Holy Spirit to come and work with you to set you free.
~Identify the persistent problems, and ask Jesus to show you where they started.
~Identify the lies you believed about yourself, other people, and God.
~Identify how you set up defenses to protect yourself from future pain.
~Ask Jesus to speak Truth into this situation.
~Confess the lies and defenses; repent from them.
~Activate your will to believe the Truth you heard from Jesus, and commit to letting that guide your life.

Our prayer is that at the first sign that you are stepping back into the bondage brought about by your past, you will call on the only name that can set you free. Then reach out to Jesus. He is always right there with you, and He loves you more than you can even imagine. He is the one your soul longs to hear speak.

The grace of our Lord Jesus Christ be with you all.

Where the Spirit of the Lord is, there is דְּרוֹר *!*

Dr. John M. Arroyo, Jr.

Dr. John M. Arroyo Jr. is a retired U.S. Army veteran from California. He is married to Angel Arroyo, and they have three children. John enlisted in the U.S. Army in 1998 and spent most of his 20-year career as a Green Beret, assigned to the 3rd Special Forces Group at Fort Bragg in North Carolina. In 2013, he was commissioned as a U.S. Army Medical Service Corps Officer. John has been deployed twice to Afghanistan and once to Iraq.

He is a survivor of the April 02, 2014, mass shooting at Fort Hood, Texas. He was treated for a gunshot wound to the neck and paralysis of the right arm at Brooke Army Medical Center in San Antonio, Texas. Doctors told John's family that they did not have a medical explanation for how he survived his injuries. It was simply a miracle! Given a second chance, John wasted no time sharing his gift and miraculous story with anyone willing to listen.

John is a highly sought-after motivational speaker known for his energetic style. He is a gifted communicator who speaks in various settings, including churches, schools, military bases, businesses, and nonprofit events. John's primary message centers around **getting up**. He illustrates this through his life experiences. He speaks about relevant issues to his audience and provides concrete solutions to real-life challenges.

John's life experiences, including addiction, failures, and disappointments, have given him a unique perspective on faith, hope, resiliency, courage, and survival. His dynamic energy, honest transparency, and vivid storytelling profoundly impact those who hear him speak, often leading to transformation and growth. His unwavering hope is grounded in his strong faith, strengthened by his deep connections with his wife, children, and extended family.

www.getupwithjohn.com

Peggy Corvin

My life verse truly tells of my life. *"I waited and waited and waited for God. At last, he looked; finally, he listened. He lifted me out of the ditch, pulled me from deep mud. He stood me up on a solid rock to make sure I wouldn't slip. He taught me how to sing the latest God-song, a praise-song to our God. More and more people are seeing this: they enter the mystery, abandoning themselves to God."*  *Psalm 40 MSG*

When He set me free, He anointed me to become a Freedom Minister using the words and ways of Jesus to encourage others to know freedom. Nothing sets my soul soaring the way seeing one of His children hear Him, discover He loves them, and claim their freedom. Even Texas sunsets pale with the glow from the countenance of the face of a newly freed brother or sister who has heard from God.

He equipped me by creating me to be a lifelong learner. I have a Bachelor's Degree and post-graduate work in Education and a Master's Degree from the King's University in Theology. He has placed me at the feet of some of the most knowledgeable Bible teachers in the body today.

He has allowed me to be a voice for freedom in the body of believers for years. Sometimes I speak, teach, or train other leaders in the process of freedom. Other times, I sit kneecap-to-kneecap with the brokenhearted until they find the courage to ask Him all their hard questions. He has always answered them with mercy, grace, and tremendous love.

I own Southwestern Legacy Press, LLC, a small publishing company focused on helping people take their God-glorifying stories and develop them into a lasting legacy. I am an author, co-author, editor, and publisher.

My husband, Stan, and I started the company seven years ago. Since Jesus recently called him home, I am continuing the work. My three children, eight grandchildren, and I miss having him here but rejoice that this is just a short separation. My prayer is that every word the Lord gives me to share will pierce the darkness that shadows over the brokenhearted.

www.swlegacypress.com
Book available on Amazon, Kindle and Audible
swlegacypress@gmail.com

Other Books By
Southwestern Legacy Press LLC

Attacked at Home!
A Green Beret's Survival Story of the Fort Hood Shooting
Captain John Arroyo, Jr. U.S. Army (Ret.)

Get Up! Get Up!: Open Their Eyes
John Arroyo, Angel Arroyo, Peggy Corvin

Diamond in the Darkness
Abused Child of Darkness, Reclaimed Daughter of Light
Peggy Corvin

Vietnam Saga
Exploits of a Combat Helicopter Pilot
Stan Corvin, Jr

Echoes of the Hunt
A Texan Told True Tale
Stan Corvin, Jr

The Eagle Above
Chronicles of an American Fighter Pilot
Stan Corvin, Jr

Adventures On Bluebonnet Ranch
Annelise Marsh and Peggy Corvin

Forged In Fire
A Lifetime of Pain Forged a Lifestyle of Resiliency
Dave Roever and Stan Corvin

Consuming Fire
A Journey of Healing Trauma's Deep Hurts
Dave Roever and Peggy Corvin

Vietnam Abyss: A Journal of Unmerited Grace
Michael Snook

Jet Pioneer: A Fighter Pilot's Memoir
MG Carl G. Schneider

I Volunteered for This
A Woman's Perspective of Serving In the U.S. Army
Theresa Benner McCullough

Made in the USA
Middletown, DE
25 September 2023

39138376R00106